ADAPTIVE TEACHING
IN PRIMARY SCHOOLS

Sara Miller McCune founded Sage Publishing in 1965 to support the dissemination of usable knowledge and educate a global community. Sage publishes more than 1000 journals and over 800 new books each year, spanning a wide range of subject areas. Our growing selection of library products includes archives, data, case studies and video. Sage remains majority owned by our founder and after her lifetime will become owned by a charitable trust that secures the company's continued independence.

Los Angeles | London | New Delhi | Singapore | Washington DC | Melbourne

ADAPTIVE TEACHING
IN PRIMARY SCHOOLS

A TOOLKIT FOR
TRAINEE TEACHERS

CHARLOTTE MOSEY
JACK STOTHARD

LM Learning Matters

1 Oliver's Yard
55 City Road
London EC1Y 1SP

2455 Teller Road
Thousand Oaks
California 91320

Unit No 323-333, Third Floor, F-Block
International Trade Tower
Nehru Place, New Delhi – 110 019

8 Marina View Suite 43-053
Asia Square Tower 1
Singapore 018960

Editor: Amy Thornton
Senior project editor: Chris Marke
Cover design: Sheila Tong
Typeset by: C&M Digitals (P) Ltd, Chennai, India

Library of Congress Control Number: 2024936724

British Library Cataloguing in Publication Data

A catalogue record for this book is available from the
British Library

ISBN 978-1-5296-7196-4
ISBN 978-1-5296-7195-7 (pbk)

DEDICATION

Charlotte Mosey: To my husband Ken for his boundless enthusiasm and encouragement. To my parents Gill and Alan and my sister Hattie for their unconditional support. To my friend and colleague Jack who has been with me on this adaptive journey. Most of all, my daughters Florence and Amelia, the inspiration for writing this book and for making me proud, always.

Jack Bryne Stothard: For my wonderful colleague Charlotte whose passion inspires me every day. For my darling nieces Agnes and Winnie – hoping that the tomorrow of education is better than today. For my dearest Granny, whose love and support is unwavering. Finally, and most importantly, for my dear parents. This book is for you.

CONTENTS

ACKNOWLEDGEMENTS

We would like to acknowledge past and current learners in schools that we have had the privilege to teach and beginning teachers at the University of Derby whom we have had the pleasure of supporting on their journeys to becoming adaptive educators.

We would also like to acknowledge our collaborative partners at Bigland Green Primary School, Tower Hamlets.

ABOUT THE AUTHORS

Charlotte Mosey is the Assistant Head of Discipline for Primary Initial Teacher Education within the Institute of Education at the University of Derby. Prior to this, she was a primary practitioner for over fifteen years, having both teaching and leadership experience throughout Key Stages 1 and 2. Charlotte has a professional interest in the teaching of English and Primary Foreign Languages, specifically focusing upon the implementation of a vibrant curriculum that is accessible for all.

Dr Jack Bryne Stothard is Assistant Programme Leader for the Doctorate of Education and leads the Teacher Education, Research and Innovation research cluster within the Institute of Education at the University of Derby. Prior to this, he was a primary school teacher and mathematics specialist with leadership experience in a variety of settings. Jack is particularly interested in pedagogic innovation and conducts research in the field of teacher education.

LIST OF ACRONYMS

BT – Beginning Teacher

CAMHS – Child and Adolescent Mental Health Services

CCF – Core Content Framework

CPD – Continuing Professional Development

DfCSF – Department for Children, Schools and Families

DfES – Department for Education and Skills

DfE – Department for Education

ECF – Early Career Framework

EEF – Education Endowment Foundation

EHCP – Education, Health and Care Plan

EYFS – Early Years Foundation Stage

ICT – Information and Communications Technology

KS1 – Key Stage 1

KS2 – Key Stage 2

MTC – Multiplication Tables Check

NACE – National Association for Able Children in Education

NC – National Curriculum

OEIF – Ofsted Education Inspection Framework

Ofsted – Office for Standards in Education, Children's Services and Skills

QTS – Qualified Teacher Status

SEN – Special Education Needs

SENCO – Special Education Needs Coordinator

TDA – Training and Development Agency

ZPD – Zone of Proximal Development

1

INTRODUCTION

By opening, reading and considering this book, you have taken the first step on your adaptive teaching journey. This book is for everyone who is curious about how to make their learning, teaching and classroom environment more adaptive, responsive and accessible. As primary school teachers and leaders, who now have the privilege of training the teachers of the future, we are passionate about sharing our thoughts and expertise on how to make learning more adaptive and inclusive. This book aims to do this, sharing our thoughts, experience and the best practice we have seen whilst reflecting upon what research and evidence also tells us.

WHAT TO EXPECT

Although much research has been conducted on the benefits of adaptive learning and teaching, all too often we believe that classrooms continue to be places where ability is seen as fixed, and a deficit model of learning is common. Equally, outdated educational practices are observed in many settings despite a wealth of evidence and research suggesting they are at least ineffective and at worst detrimental to the academic and personal wellbeing of learners. This book explores and addresses 'lethal mutations' in education, a term made famous by Edward Haertel (Brown and Campione, 1996). We define lethal mutations as positive and effective evidence-based practices and thinking which has become harmful due to small or larger changes or adaptations when translated into practice. This will be explored in relation to mindsets surrounding differentiation and practices such as ability grouping.

Each chapter in this toolkit offers an insight into a specific aspect of educational practice and thinking. However, we recognise that some of the topics and ideas discussed will overlap. This is true in cases such as grouping and environments as well as assessment and questioning.

Whilst researching and creating this toolkit, as writers we have also been on our own adaptive learning and teaching journey, and we had not anticipated the impact this process would have on our own practice. Indeed, we started planning this book with specific chapters in mind which followed a certain running order, commencing with a focus on implementation of strategies. However, we now recognise the importance of assessment as a starting point in the adaptive learning journey, therefore this is the first element in our toolkit. Our discussion linked to assessment (Chapter 2) will help you to consider this common practice in a new way with a focus on adapting learning, the importance of formative practice and having a robust understanding as to what we should be assessing in terms of specific knowledge and skills.

It could be argued that flexible grouping is at the very heart of adaptive teaching; evidence shows that fixed ability grouping can be detrimental to learners. Boaler et al. (2000) found that ability grouping restricts opportunity of learning and often leads to learners constructing themselves as failures. Chapter 3 will offer practical ideas to support the implementation of creative grouping in the classroom and give support for overcoming the very real fears around a shifting mindset in learning environments and the often-overwhelming challenge of meeting the needs of diverse learners.

We recognise how essential culture is in a school to ensure learners can be supported to grow and develop to their full potential. Often, in schools there is a disproportionate emphasis on teaching; the learning environment and culture within a school are secondary concerns. Focusing on learning environments, Chapter 4 develops on our previous work (Mosey and Stothard, 2022), considering how creating adaptive learning environments and learning experiences are imperative when implementing responsive practice.

Effective scaffolding and modelling is a key element of an adaptive learning environment; in Chapter 5 we reflect upon walking the scaffolding 'tight-rope', the importance of how a teacher must provide effective modelling and support whilst guiding their learners to be confident in their own ability, to be able to work independently and with others and, importantly, experiencing success regardless of ability.

Quality-first teaching is the foundation of any adaptive classroom and assessment informs all interventions that may be required, such as long-term programmes to reduce gaps in knowledge or responsive and *in the moment* support in a lesson. Chapter 6 reflects upon the ethical dilemmas faced by the practitioner; whether it is in the best interest of a learner to be withdrawn from their peer group for the extra input and who is best placed to provide the support are just two considerations.

Learning does not happen in a vacuum and there are many factors which influence how well the learning process takes place. In Chapter 7, Cognition and Metacognition, we think about how cognition can help us develop adaptive pedagogical practices. Moreover, we consider how metacognitive themes can help us to encourage our learners to take control of their own learning and assess themselves throughout the process.

Finally, questioning is one of the most common but important practices that teachers engage in daily. Asking questions is vital to adapting our learning and teaching so we have dedicated the whole of Chapter 8 to understanding this. Not only is it important for teachers to develop their practice of questioning, we also show how learners can improve their own ability to question and why this is so important for learning and teaching.

DIFFERENTIATION AND ADAPTIVE TEACHING

'Differentiation' has become a contentious term in recent years as policy and guidance has challenged its effectiveness; however, practical and specific alternatives to the traditional approaches of differentiation are elusive, despite the terminology of adaptive teaching being used in a range of documents.

Deunk et al. (2018) explore how differentiation can be defined and settle upon the notion that the approach can include a number of strategies including grouping, regular assessment, adaptive resources, modifying activities and providing different learning opportunities depending on ability. In classrooms, differentiation is seen in many guises and as an umbrella approach clearly has many elements; however, the most controversial is grouping by ability owing to the belief that teachers may have unconsciously lower expectations of less able pupils. Despite government guidance calling for a stronger sense of adaptation rather than artificial grouping, many principles of traditional differentiation are still implemented as part of a school approach, including ability grouping.

Tomlinson (2001) defines differentiation as:

- proactive;

- centred around quality over quantity;

- providing multiple approaches to content, process and product;

- student-centred;

- a blend of whole-class, group and individual instruction;

- dynamic.

As a concept, differentiation, according to Tomlinson (2001), appears to be inclusive and responsive to individual needs. However, we strongly feel that this approach has been diluted and become a pseudo-practice which does not resemble what was intended by Tomlinson's research. Again, this is a type of lethal mutations, a practice which has been altered and has become ineffective. Adaptive teaching should be seen as a catalyst for change; the traditional culture of differentiation is no longer fit for purpose because you cannot realistically accommodate the huge range of diversity including academic, personal, social and emotional experiences that our learners bring into the classroom.

Based on our experience and research, we believe that adaptive teaching is:

- a change of mindset and culture towards truly inclusive practice;

- a shift in thinking about what learners can do, rather than what they cannot;

- underpinned by ongoing, rigorous formative assessment;

- responsive and intuitive practice;

- based on excellent knowledge of the curriculum and a range of pedagogical approaches;

- focused on the process of learning rather than teaching.

Adaptive teaching should be recognised as a progression from the traditional approaches of differentiation (often acknowledged as artificial grouping and setting different tasks), based firmly upon the foundations of quality-first teaching and the notion that all learners, regardless of ability, should have the opportunity to meet common goals and high expectations.

As published schemes in core areas of teaching have started to dominate (if not saturate) the market and with the national curriculum (DfE, 2013a) offering a course of study for a year group regardless of individual need, ways in which to adapt the curriculum to suit the needs of all learners are increasingly important. Headline facts and figures for the academic year 2022/3 provide an insight into the trend of increases linked to the number of children having special educational needs (SEN) since 2016. Currently there are 1,187,384 pupils in England who are recognised as having SEN support without an education, health and care plan (EHCP), up from 4.7 per cent in 2022. There are 389,171 pupils who have an EHCP, equating to 4.3 per cent of pupils. Again, this is up by 4.0 per cent since 2022. This will be explored further in Chapter 3, Grouping.

As more children are identified as having specific learning needs in mainstream classrooms, teachers need to be able to respond to their requirements effectively, providing an inclusive learning environment for all. Historically, it could be argued that differentiation often resulted in unaspiring expectations for lower-attaining learners, with children being grouped in a fixed way and not having the opportunity to demonstrate their understanding fully. Low-attaining learners grouped together with a task that does not provide a level of challenge or does not take into consideration their strengths and previous learning experiences could be limited by a glass-ceiling of potential. As can be seen in Figure 1.1, many teachers believe that grouping inherently gives learners the possibility of moving throughout the groups depending on their level of need. To the left of the diagram, under intention, groups appear to be interlinked and learners can move between the groups. As shown in reality, on the right, our experience and research from collaborating with schools demonstrates the opposite: groups of learners do not move between the groups and have little or no opportunity to do so. Over time, groups become increasingly distant and separated. Consider how many of your learners have moved into a different ability group during your time in a school?

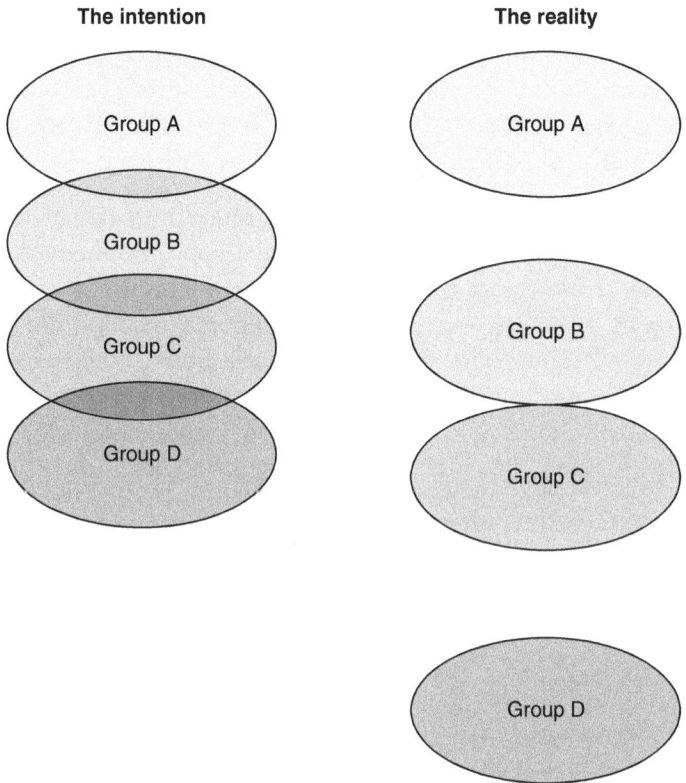

Figure 1.1   Unintended disparities caused by ability grouping

ADAPTIVE TEACHING: TURNING POLICY INTO PRACTICE

Adaptive teaching promotes the importance of maintaining high standards for all, regardless of ability – rather than offering three different activities, the learning should be separated into distinct parts and recognised as steps to success, the objective or end goal should be the same but the journey to success will be different for all learners. Using robust targeted strategies including pre-teaching and metacognitive approaches is beneficial; teaching assistants can also be pivotal to scaffolding learning effectively and providing timely interventions. The EEF *Guidance Report* (2021) highlights how TAs should not be used as a supportive resource for low attainers alone; rather leaders should be directing them towards providing systematic and targeted support with the overarching intention to improve attainment throughout the school.

The *Special Educational Needs and Disabilities Code of Practice* (2015) highlights that differentiation is indeed an expectation: 'High quality teaching that is differentiated and personalised will meet the individual needs of the majority of children and young people' (DfE, 2015, 1.24). There will be times when it is, of course, appropriate for teachers to provide different outcomes to suit individuals as a result of specifically identified SEN requirements; however, Ofsted and the DfE are very clear that they do not require teachers to create differentiated tasks for every lesson. Instead, it is promoted that schools will provide a level of support so that all pupils can achieve the learning outcomes.

In January 2019, Ofsted published an overview of research in their *Education Inspection Framework*, which highlighted that differentiation through different teaching activities or resources did not demonstrate a significant impact upon pupils' outcomes; however, adapting teaching by providing focused support to pupils who are not making progress is likely to improve outcomes. The report states that adaptive teaching should be clearly distinguished from forms of differentiation that cause teachers to artificially create distinct tasks for different groups of pupils or to set lower expectations for particular pupils (Ofsted, 2019).

The *Teachers' Standards* (2021) offer the minimum level of practice expected of trainees and teachers from their award of qualified teacher status (QTS). Standard 5, 'Adapt teaching to respond to the strengths and needs of all pupils', includes the statement, 'know when and how to differentiate appropriately, using approaches which enable pupils to be taught effectively' (DfE, 2021, p.11). The main message here is how to adapt teaching to support various stages of development and, most importantly, have a secure knowledge of the children that you teach. Interestingly, the *Early Career Framework* (ECF) (DfE, 2019a) – specifically Standard 5 entitled 'Adaptive Teaching' – offers a more in-depth and considered outline of what adaptive teaching can look like in reality and critically; the way in which this document references adaptive teaching rather than differentiation is significant. Published in 2019 by the DfE, it fundamentally provides a framework for what early career teachers are entitled to learn about and learn how to do when they commence their journey as practitioners. It also supports the entitlement of two years of professional development bridging the gap between initial teacher training/education and their professional career as a practitioner.

The framework is divided into five core areas of teaching, behaviour management, pedagogy, curriculum, assessment and professional behaviours; these are subdivided into eight standards linked to the *Teachers' Standards*. Within Standard 5, it is made clear that adaptive teaching should not be a mechanism to provide different tasks for distinct groups or an excuse for lower expectations for specific pupils (DfE, 2019a).

This document is a good starting point for practitioners to consider the context in which they are working. Essentially, the message is clear, adapting in a responsive way, by providing targeted support, understanding the needs of your pupils, avoiding distinct tasks for different groups, flexibly grouping in order to offer tailored support but with the caveat that this must be monitored carefully, using teaching assistants effectively and planning to connect new learning with existing knowledge. Ultimately, applying high expectations for all and ensuring that the curriculum is rich and balanced is essential.

The *Initial Teacher Training (ITT): Core Content Framework* (CCF) (DfE, 2019b) provides the minimum entitlement for all trainee teachers and provides a basis on which to begin thinking about adaptive teaching. Adaptive Teaching (Standard 5 – 'Adapt teaching') states beginning teachers should learn that:

- pupils are likely to learn at different rates and to require different levels and types of support from teachers to succeed;

- seeking to understand pupils' differences, including their different levels of prior knowledge and potential barriers to learning, is an essential part of teaching;

- adapting teaching in a responsive way, including by providing targeted support to pupils who are struggling, is likely to increase pupil success;

- adaptive teaching is less likely to be valuable if it causes the teacher to artificially create distinct tasks for different groups of pupils or to set lower expectations for particular pupils;

- flexibly grouping pupils within a class to provide more tailored support can be effective, but care should be taken to monitor its impact on engagement and motivation, particularly for low-attaining pupils;

- there is a common misconception that pupils have distinct and identifiable learning styles. This is not supported by evidence and attempting to tailor lessons to learning styles is unlikely to be beneficial;

- pupils with SEN or disabilities are likely to require additional or adapted support; working closely with colleagues, families and pupils to understand barriers and identify effective strategies is essential.

SO, THE ADAPTIVE JOURNEY BEGINS ...

Imagine an adaptive classroom that is accessible and open to everyone. Think of this space as a community of learners in which everyone can learn, grow and achieve together.

Draw sketches of your ideas or make a list of what comes to mind when you think about an adaptive classroom environment; we will return to your reflection at the end of this book.

2

ASSESSMENT

CHAPTER OBJECTIVES

After engaging with this chapter, you will be able to:

- understand what assessment is and the different types of assessment used;
- understand the policy implications of assessment in adaptive teaching;
- be able to apply principles of assessment to your own practice;
- consider strategies for assessing different types of knowledge.

INTRODUCTION

Assessment is a strange and baffling aspect of teaching and learning. It is both superfluous and yet absolutely essential for teaching. Superfluous because much of our assessment practice focuses on teaching rather than learning, but absolutely essential to the development of our learners' understanding. Dylan Wiliam famously noted that if students learnt what they were taught, we wouldn't need to assess them. But as every teacher knows, students do not learn what we teach them. We will discuss this in more detail in this chapter, specifically in relation to what we intend our students to learn, what happens during the process of learning and what is actually learnt. We can think of this as the intention, the action and the result of our learning and teaching practice. This means assessment is essential if we are truly able to understand this. A nice quote given by Child and Ellis (2021) can help us think about assessment as 'the process of collecting evidence with respect to something we want to know more about' (p. 8). The definition gives us a very general point from which we begin our conversation about assessment. Before beginning to engage with this chapter, consider the following statements to gauge your current views on assessment:

'Assessment should take place in every lesson'

'Assessment and testing are the same thing'

'Examinations are the only type of assessment that matter'

'Assessment is a one-way process: teachers give students feedback about their work'

'Work should always be given a grade or mark'

POLICY

Of course, as teachers we are advised on how to assess learning in our classroom through policy. One of the most important ways this is revealed is through the DfE's *Teachers' Standards* (2021) and the *Initial Teacher Education (ITT): Core Content Framework* (CCF) (2019b). Teachers' Standard 6: 'Make accurate and productive use of assessment' offers guidance on practices for assessing learning for teachers including:

- know and understand how to assess the relevant subject and curriculum areas, including statutory assessment requirements;

- make use of formative and summative assessment to secure pupils' progress;

- use relevant data to monitor progress, set targets, and plan subsequent lessons;

- give pupils regular feedback, both orally and through accurate marking, and encourage pupils to respond to the feedback.

CCF Standard 6: Assessment (Teachers' Standard 6 – 'Make accurate and productive use of assessment') offers further guidance for beginning teachers suggesting they should:

Learn that …

1. Effective assessment is critical to teaching because it provides teachers with information about pupils' understanding and needs.

2. Good assessment helps teachers avoid being over-influenced by potentially misleading factors, such as how busy pupils appear.

3. Before using any assessment, teachers should be clear about the decision it will be used to support and be able to justify its use.

4. To be of value, teachers use information from assessments to inform the decisions they make; in turn, pupils must be able to act on feedback for it to have an effect.

5. High-quality feedback can be written or verbal; it is likely to be accurate and clear, encourage further effort, and provide specific guidance on how to improve.

6. Over time, feedback should support pupils to monitor and regulate their own learning.

7. Working with colleagues to identify efficient approaches to assessment is important; assessment can become onerous and have a disproportionate impact on workload.

The Office for Standards in Education, Children's Services and Skills (Ofsted) also provides some details regarding assessment and its expectations towards schools with regards to the quality and practice of assessment. In its most recent copy of the inspection framework (2023a), assessment is mentioned scarcely (only 40 times). Some important points to remember are:

- Ofsted states it will not advocate a particular method of assessment (27);

- the extent to which teachers use assessment to check pupils' understanding to inform teaching, and to help pupils embed key concepts, use knowledge fluently and develop their understanding, and not simply memorise disconnected facts (227);

- Ofsted will discuss with staff whether assessment practices create any unnecessary burdens (254);

- inspectors will consider whether the ongoing assessment of pupils' phonics progress is sufficiently frequent and detailed (260).

Equally, in Ofsted's grade descriptors for quality of education (2019b), assessment is only mentioned in the Good (2) grading boundary, but not in Outstanding (1), Requires Improvement (3) or Inadequate (4). It states:

> **Good (2)** – *'Teachers and leaders use assessment well. For example, they use it to help pupils embed and use knowledge fluently, or to check understanding and inform teaching, or to understand different starting points and gaps as a result of the COVID-19 pandemic. Leaders understand the limitations of assessment and do not use it in a way that creates unnecessary burdens on staff or pupils.'*

This lack of clarity regarding assessment often means teachers and school leaders are left to guess and invent their own individual approaches to assessment in their schools. In doing so they attempt to meet Ofsted's expectations due to fear of a poor inspection grading. However, this also means there is a great deal of flexibility around how schools can approach assessment. Adapting whole-school assessment to the individual needs of your learners in your context can be a powerful way of ensuring that assessment is being used well in the eyes of Ofsted.

SUMMATIVE VS FORMATIVE ASSESSMENT

The field of assessment is vast and much has been written on this area. That said, some common language is used to articulate what we mean by assessment. Broadly, we can separate assessment into two areas; however, it is good to bear in mind there will be some overlap.

SUMMATIVE ASSESSMENT AND ADAPTIVE TEACHING

Summative assessments are often utilised at the end of a learning period, such as a unit of work, a topic, or a year. Whilst summative assessments are important for understanding the attainment of a learner, they are not particularly useful for understanding the process of learning. More importantly, summative assessment is not particularly useful for adapting day-to-day learning and teaching. We can consider a standardised test such as the SATs (completed in Year 6) or the statutory multiplication tables check (MTC, completed in Year 4) as a type of statutory assessment, but these kinds of assessments reveal little about what learners have understood and more about what they have remembered, retained and, finally, attained. Equally, because they are administered after the learning has taken place, they are ineffective as tools for adapting our learning and teaching. They are, however, useful as part of a wider assessment process for understanding learners' progress across a longer period of time. Of course, not all summative assessment is the same but there are some commonalities.

1. *An end-point assessment.* Typically, summative assessments are utilised after the learning has taken place to evaluate how well learners have understood something. As such, they cannot help teachers understand how they can adapt or change their learning strategies or pedagogical approach directly in relation to the material being taught. They can help teachers to reflect on the overall effectiveness of pedagogical approaches in the classroom in some respects but this does not entail a holistic way of thinking about education.

2. *A system of ranking and grading.* Because summative assessment necessarily always involves assigning a grade to measure achievement, it is a process of grading and ranking individuals and schools and is the main process by which schools are measured in league tables. These assessments also are usually used when completing academic records for learners. As such, they are mainly concerned with assessing teaching, and not learning.

3. *High stakes and pressurised.* On a social and emotional level, summative assessment can be extremely stressful for both learners and teachers due to being high stakes for both parties. There are consequences for both teachers and learners based on summative assessment. For students, these assessments can lead to academic and emotional consequences such as shame or a lack of confidence which can remain with a learner for a very long time, if not their entire educational journey. For teachers, such assessments can be used to judge their ability and efficacy as a teacher, affecting progression and opportunities. Summative assessments can determine our educational trajectory in many ways.

4. *Tools for accountability.* Often summative assessments are used not as a tool for improving learning and teaching but as a tool for accountability. They are used less often to measure the effectiveness of pedagogical approaches or initiatives and more usually to assess individuals and schools. Statutory tests, such as SATs and the MTC mentioned above are necessarily used to compare and contrast education outcomes across schools in England. Therefore, they are less useful for adapting learning and teaching and more useful for comparing education outcomes.

FORMATIVE ASSESSMENT AND ADAPTIVE TEACHING

Whilst summative assessment tends to take place at the end of a learning phase, formative assessment takes place throughout the learning phase. It could be said that formative assessment never ends. It is a form of ongoing evaluation in relation to the learning that is taking place in a classroom. It is important because it helps teachers and learners understand where they are in relation to the learning that is taking place and how best the intervention can be adapted to meet individual learners' needs. It is an engaging and focused activity which enables teachers to understand exactly what has been learnt throughout a learning process, rather than what they think has been learnt. As Dylan Wiliam noted, because learners do not learn what we teach, formative assessment is indispensable to understanding how the enacted process of learning led to formation of concepts understanding and, more importantly, misconceptions which need to be addressed. There is no end to the kinds of activities which can be used as part of formative assessment practice, including but not limited to: discussions, quizzes, verbal feedback, peer feedback, observations, games etc. Contrary to summative assessment, which is incredibly low in terms of student participation, learners are actively included in this process so that they might better understand how they can further improve their own understanding and debug misconceptions that might be present. Again, some commonalities of formative assessment are as follows.

1. *It is ongoing and continuous.* It could be argued that, within a classroom, formative assessment never stops taking place. Whilst the practice of this type of assessment may be taking place more obviously and explicitly in an assessment activity, it is likely it is also taking place quite implicitly, through homing in on conversations or noticing what learners are doing. Therefore, it makes up a huge part of a teacher's day-to-day activity and is essential for adaptive learning and teaching. This also means that timely intervention may take place at any time and usually when it is most needed.

2. *It is focused on feeding forward.* The main focus of formative assessment is to provide information that can be utilised in the future. It is a practice concerned with the future and progress but happens in a timely and efficient way. Therefore, it informs learners and teachers about current levels of understanding and skill so this might be improved in the future. We can see how summative assessment conducted at the end of a learning period cannot do this and thus does not function to adapt learning and teaching.

3. *It is student-focused.* In opposition to summative assessment, which rarely involves the learner in the process apart from completing an assessment, formative practices actively constitute the learner as a partner in the process. This can be done in various ways, often involving encouraging students to reflect and think about their learning and the learning of others around them. Reflect on a time when a teacher asked you to look at something you had done or think about it differently when compared to another student. This autonomy can be a powerful tool also in our classrooms. We will discuss this in more detail in Chapter 7, Cognition and metacognition.

4. *It is diagnostic in nature.* Whilst we have argued that summative assessment functions to grade and categorise learners, formative assessment has no ability to do so because it is purely diagnostic in nature. One can understand formative assessment as the process of identifying strengths, weaknesses, or needs of an individual learner or a group so that adaptations can be made.

5. *Most importantly, its purpose is to adapt learning and teaching.* Finally, formative assessment functions to help us understand how we might adapt our strategies and approaches to learning. I have observed excellent teaching where learners are brought together as a whole class after a teacher has noticed a common misconception as well as individual targeted support for learners who may need scaffolding. Not only does this enable a teacher to adapt and change their approach to learning and teaching but, if a teacher is engaging in continuous formative assessment, this can be done in a timely if not immediate way. Excellent assessment occurs when a teacher can provide instantaneous intervention for a learner to prevent them developing misconceptions and develop and grow their confidence. This has relevance because the intended objects of learning and the actual learning often are not the same thing (this will be discussed below).

REFLECTIVE ACTIVITY

Look at the following types of assessment which may commonly take place in the classroom in a range of curriculum subjects. For each, decide whether you think they are formative or summative in nature:

- a standardised test paper;

- learners marking the learning of their peers;

- engaging in a classroom discussion;

- giving verbal feedback to a learner on an exercise they have completed;

- offering learners a misconception to discuss which was common in the class;

- an interactive quiz completed in partnership with other learners;

- learners showing a solution on a whiteboard;

- a plenary exercise at the end of a lesson.

TYPES OF ASSESSMENT

Now we understand the difference between summative and formative assessment, we can contextualise this within the three most common types of assessment found in the classroom: assessment for/of/as learning. Assessment *of* learning, or summative assessment, has already been discussed above and we shall discuss assessment *as* learning in Chapter 7, focusing on metacognition and cognition. However, here are some practical examples of the types of activities which might be included in these three types of assessment in the classroom:

Table 2.1   *Practical examples of the types of activities*

Assessment of learning Summative assessment	Assessment *for* learning Formative assessment	Assessment as learning Student reflection
Mr Thomas is teaching a Year 4 class and they have just started a unit on fractions. To further understand what his learners already know he decides to give them a short assessment. They want to know exactly what each learner knows individually so they ask the learners to do the assessment individually and in silence so they can concentrate properly. At the end of the unit of work they give the learners the same paper so they can compare the differences between their earlier performance and after the unit of work. They are happy because they can see an improvement in the marks which have been attained by the learners. However, they notice some gaps remain in their learners' understanding, but Mr Thomas needs to move onto the next unit of learning and makes a note to revisit this when time allows. The grades are recorded by Mr Thomas and shared with the senior leadership team, including the mathematics lead and key stage leader. They are also used as part of their performance management review at the end of the year.	Mrs Jahn is teaching a Year 1 class, and they are starting to learn about wild and garden plants, including trees in science. They want to know what their learners already know about the topic. Mrs Jahn sets up an activity by putting up lots of different images of plants and trees for learners to look at as well as a range of plant materials they have collected. They allow the learner to handle and discuss the materials and make notes about what they witnessed. Drawing the learner together they engage in further discussion and Mrs Jahn uses this information to plan how they will teach the topic. In each lesson they use carefully crafted learning experiences to expose the common misconceptions they are aware of from their subject knowledge and challenge learners to deepen the concepts. As the topic continues, Mrs Jahn uses a range of different strategies to help learners understand including peer- and self-assessment. In and out of science lessons they ask the children about things they have noticed and what they can remember and encourage learners to discuss when outside.	Mrs O'Neil is teaching a Year 6 class, and they are working on a topic focusing on Central American geography. They are trying to incorporate assessment as learning into their strategies to promote engagement and motivation. They ask the children to evaluate what they already know about this topic with a KWL grid: what I know, what I want to know and what I have learnt. Each lesson this grid is revisited so learners can actively reflect on the progress they are making and where improvements might be made. They are asked to reflect on this with their peers and come up with some goals and strategies on how they will achieve this. They are also given independent time to conduct their own research and learning. At the end of the lesson, they are asked to update their grid again and reflect on their learning success. Mrs O'Neil continually encourages the learners to take responsibility for their own learning and prioritise what is important and interesting for them to learn.

━━ REFLECTIVE ACTIVITY ━━━

As learners, there are aspects of learning and teaching that we may like or dislike or that we feel may be effective or ineffective. Consider the three examples above and consider which is most suited to you as a learner. Are there aspects of each example which speak to you whilst others do not? Consider these as you continue reading the rest of the chapter, as well as how you might integrate these into your own practice.

TYPES OF KNOWLEDGE TO BE ASSESSED

Once we have understood the types of assessment that may be taking place in an adaptive learning environment, it is also important to think about the kinds of knowledge or understanding that we are assessing in the classroom. This is important because we need to know *what* we want our learners to know, we need to know *how* we will be teaching this and also reflect on *what* learners have actually learnt. We can understand this as being what we intend for our students to learn (the intended), how they learn this (the enacted) and what they actually learn (the learnt). There are three ways of doing this. Consider the case study below from a mathematics lesson:

━━ CASE STUDY ━━

Mr Farrah's learners are thinking about long division as part of their lesson. He wants learners to have a good understanding of how the algorithm works but recognises this is a complex mathematical concept. He has a good knowledge of long division as he has taught it for many years. Mr Farrah knows that the learners need to have a good understanding of column subtraction, multiplication facts and other skills. Mr Farrah models the process for the learners and then asks them to discuss this together. He uses a variety of pedagogical approaches such as 'I do, you do', modelling, guided practice and peer discussion. Finally, he comes to reflect on what has been learnt and finds that many have misunderstood the process and have become confused with the mixture of multiplication and subtraction techniques as part of this division work. He seeks advice from other colleagues as the lesson seemed to go well and learners were demonstrating understanding. He also felt his teaching and pedagogical approach fitted well with the class as they were engaged and enthusiastic.

THREE TYPES OF LEARNING

The example above demonstrates that in adapting our learning and teaching we have to consider different types of understanding and what we are *actually* assessing. Sadly, all too often in schools, teachers focus on assessing the intended objects of knowledge and neglect the learnt objects of knowledge and the role the enacted process has in this.

The intended learning – this refers to the actual concepts or skills we wish our learners to become familiar with. We can also call this knowledge the *intended curriculum*. The *National Curriculum in England* (DfE, 2013b) is taught in all local authority-maintained schools and used by many schools as a basis for planning what will be taught in schools. In the above example, Mr Farrah has identified a key mathematical skill (dividing) which learners are to become familiar with.

The enacted learning – is the process in which the learning takes places. We often refer to this as the *pedagogical knowledge* or *pedagogical process* through which learning takes place. Schulman (1986) described the way in which certain approaches to learning can make the process simpler or more difficult. He said:

> *Pedagogical content knowledge also includes an understanding of what makes the learning of specific topics easy or difficult: the conceptions and preconceptions that students of different ages and backgrounds bring with them to the learning of those most frequently taught topics and lessons. (p. 9)*

For example, using extremely abstract and complicated language and diagrams with younger learners is likely to be less effective than using simpler language and pictures to help them understand something. As we can see in the above example, we can tailor our pedagogical content knowledge well to our learners but sometimes it is not always completely effective to support concept acquisition. That's why immediate formative assessment is so important for adapting our learning strategies.

The learnt – is what is *actually learnt* in the lesson, not what we think was. We must remember as teachers this can be very different from what we intended to be learnt and, as such, this is the main place in which assessment must take place. It is often difficult for teachers to do this for two reasons. Firstly, because it can be a difficult process emotionally to realise our learners have 'missed the point' or learnt something incorrectly, it may lead to feelings of disappointment and affect self-esteem. However, this is not necessarily a negative thing. We must remember that concept acquisition must essentially go through many phases which are necessarily incomplete or inaccurate before a solid and complete conceptual understand is formed. Secondly, because it is very difficult to uncover in great detail exactly what has been learnt. This will be explored in more detail shortly when we consider that learners express their understanding in tacit and explicit forms. As we can see in the example above, throughout a lesson we may be receiving lots of positive signs that learners are understanding what we are teaching. Learners may be motivated and engaged, they may be giving correct solutions to questions and look 'busy', but this does not guarantee that the intended and actually learnt knowledge is the same thing. Therefore, when adapting our learning and teaching, we must remember these three types of knowledge may need to be adapted and assessed.

TACIT VS EXPLICIT KNOWLEDGE

When engaging in assessment practices to adapt our learning and teaching, we also have to consider the types of knowledge that we are trying to assess. For example, philosopher and scientist Karl Polanyi (1891–1976) argued that there two knowledges we need to remember. Let us begin with the easier to observe and assess (*explicit*) and then move on to the more complex (*tacit*).

EXPLICIT KNOWLEDGE

Explicit knowledge is easier for teachers to assess because it is tangible and easily expressed. This means learners can make this knowledge known to teachers more easily through language, writing, numbers and other means. It uses common symbols and communication to make it known to others. Some features of explicit knowledge are:

- *It is easily expressed and communicated.* We can write this kind of knowledge down in words or numbers which other people can see and understand as well. For example, we can express this kind of knowledge through writing in an English lesson or showing a calculation in mathematics lesson. This means it can be easily shared with other learners and teachers so they might understand this knowledge too. The ideas in this book can be shared easily with other educationalists because we are using the shared language of English to put our ideas across.

- *Explicit knowledge is underpinned by tacit knowledge.* Polanyi argued that much of our explicit knowledge is underpinned by our tacit knowledge. Moreover, much of our tacit knowledge may not be easily transformed into explicit knowledge. As such, it becomes more difficult as a teacher to try and engage with such knowledge.

TACIT KNOWLEDGE

This knowledge refers to what cannot be easily expressed or shared with others. This is because there is no formal or common way to share such knowledge because it is experiential. It is subjective and likely relates to the life experiences of a learner. We can understand by trying to explain to someone what the feeling of happiness is without using the word happiness. It becomes clear that formal language cannot always adequately express what a feeling of happiness is actually like. Equally, if we are able to express such an experience in words or symbols, it can be easily misread or misunderstood by others. In an educational context, tacit knowledge cannot be easily understood or assessed by teachers unless we can express it more explicitly.

- *It is often non-verbal and implicit.* As teachers often use language and discussion as a means to assess and adapt learning and teaching, tacit knowledge is complex because it cannot be easily translated into language to share. Thus, teachers must think of creative and different ways of encouraging tacit knowledge to be exposed so it might be assessed. It might easily be embedded in the actions and personal experiences of a learner, meaning that a teacher must have creative ways of assessing this. The skill of riding a bike exemplifies tacit knowledge. Whilst one can explain the mechanisms of riding a bike, it is the experience of riding which allows the skill to form.

- *It is context-dependent.* Because tacit knowledge is developed through experience and practice it is also dependent on context. This means it is likely to be difficult to translate such experience easily into other contexts. We can certainly see this when writers find it difficult to use certain punctuation when writing in other subjects, even though they consistently use them in English. This may be because their knowledge is context-dependent and intricately linked to their personal experience of certain information.

- *It is skill-based.* Tacit knowledge often involves skills, expertise and know-how that individuals acquire through practice and experience. This can include motor skills, craftsmanship, or intuitive problem-solving abilities.

- *It is hard to teach and assess.* As tacit knowledge is difficult to articulate in formalised ways, it becomes more challenging to teach in ways which are commonly seen in schools. Particular pedagogical strategies or methods which are used by schools may often be ineffective because they are not useful in teaching such tacit knowledge. Equally, because they cannot be easily translated into a formalised coding, such as words and numerals, it becomes harder for teachers to assess such knowledge. However, because tacit knowledge forms the basis of explicit knowledge, it is crucial we have some strategies to explore this kind of knowledge.

REFLECTIVE ACTIVITY

Reflect on a lesson you have recently taught or a lesson you plan on teaching in the near future. As part of this lesson, you will want your learners to secure a range of skills and knowledge.

Make a list of which knowledge you will be teaching in this lesson and consider what tacit and explicit knowledge you will need to be aware of.

Consider the examples above to help you think about this.

THE JOHARI WINDOW

As has been discussed, the intended, enacted and learnt within a lesson is so important when assessing understanding and adapting learning and teaching. We have argued this is because, in many ways, what has been learnt by students is hidden for us. This can be exemplified by an innovative use of the Johari window model which we shall discuss now in relation to educational assessment. Luft and Ingham (1955) developed the Johari window as a method for understanding a person's awareness of themselves and others in terms of their personality, communication style and interpersonal relationships. We can apply this to education and, specifically, assessment to help us think about the relationship between ourselves and our learners and what they know. In particular, it can help us think about how we can come to know exactly what a student has learnt rather than focusing on what we think they have learnt based on our intended learning and the enacted process. The Johari window has four areas named by Luft and Ingham as:

- *open*: what is known by both individuals;

- *hidden*: what is known by one individual but is hidden from another. This area is common when individuals do not want to share something about themselves;

- *blindspot* (*intervention*): what is known to the other but not to the individual themselves. Receiving intervention and feedback is essential;

- *unknown*: information that is unknown to both individuals. It is information that is undiscovered but has huge implications for potential that is yet to be discovered or explored.

	Known to the teacher	Not known to the teacher
Known to the learner	Open: mainly explicit knowledge	Hidden: mainly tacit knowledge
Not known to the learner	Intervention: mainly explicit knowledge	Unknown: mainly tacit knowledge

Figure 2.1   The Johari window of assessment

The goal of the engaging with the Johari window is to think of assessment as a tool to increase the open quadrant where both the learner and the teacher has understood the actual learnt objects of knowledge. Here are some examples and strategies of how to use the Johari window for developing your assessment practice along with corresponding reference to the CCF for beginning teachers (DfE, 2019b):

OPEN

When in the open quadrant both the learner and the teacher know what has actually been learnt. It is likely that this form of knowledge is explicit because the learner has expressed it in a way that can be clearly understood. This being the case, there is great opportunity to push forward a learner's understanding.

Example: imagine a learner is understanding the difference between a mammal and a fish in a science lesson. They have engaged with the intended learning and developed a good understanding. They feel confident because they can express what they understand to their teacher and have identified common misconceptions and important points of difference through a learning experience. The teacher is confident the learner can be pushed on to broaden and deepen their understanding. The teacher is able to adapt and respond to this situation due to having a clear understanding of the actually learnt knowledge of the student.

Strategies:

- focusing on specific targets to move learners forward will be important here and continuing to reflect on what they have learnt through ongoing formative assessment (CCF 6);

- using expert subject knowledge to consider how learners might master specific concepts and knowledge through further opportunity and assessment (CCF 3);

- ensuring high-quality feedback continues to be offered from yourself as a teacher but also from peers (CCF 6).

HIDDEN

When the object learnt is hidden this means it is known by the learner but not by the teacher. This suggests tacit knowledge is involved and it could be that it is difficult for the learner to express or communicate what they have learnt or understood. It is important that the teacher uses strategies to reduce what is hidden from them. This can often come about due to teachers focusing too much on the intended curriculum and not on what has actually been learnt.

Example: in the same science lesson a learner has engaged with a learning experience to show they understand the difference between mammals and fish. They have completed the task correctly and the teacher has seen they have successfully done this, surmising they have an understanding of the difference. However, this is not the case. The learner still has doubts and misconceptions regarding the intended learning and has merely been successful in the task. This is because their misconceptions, based on tacit experience of the difference between fish and mammals, has not been exposed in this instance; there is no specialised adaptation to the learning strategy as the learnt knowledge is hidden – the teacher believes the intended learning has been achieved.

Strategies:

- focusing on different ways to uncover tacit knowledge will be crucial to ensure the teacher can understand what has been learnt so they can adapt their learning and teaching strategies. Using a range of different approaches, such as dialogue (Alexander, 2020) and observation (Palaiologou, 2019) of learners' thoughts and actions may make what has been learnt more obvious, especially knowledge in tacit form;

- relying on other colleagues – expert colleagues and colleagues within the classroom, such as a teaching assistant or partner teacher – will be useful to further understand what has been learnt from another perspective (CCF 7);

- using a range of high-quality questioning (as discussed in Chapter 8, Questioning) will be essential for exploring the thinking and understanding of the learner. Recalcitrant questioning can also be particularly effective for identifying misconceptions in a learner's understanding.

INTERVENTION

When in the intervention quadrant the teacher has understood what has been learnt by the learner, but the learner may not understand or has developed a misconception with regards to the intended learning. However, due to the teacher's expert curriculum and subject knowledge they can identify the best way to address these issues by adapting their pedagogical content knowledge for the individual learner. It is also important to remember that, sometimes, teachers can perpetuate or even teach misconceptions without meaning to (Stothard, 2021).

Example: in the same science lesson a learner has engaged with a learning experience to show they understand the difference between mammals and fish. On this occasion, the learner has demonstrated their misconceptions and lack of confidence in the activity which has been swiftly noticed by the teacher due to their formative assessment practice. The teacher knows what has actually been learnt, which is not the intended learning, and is able to adequately adapt their learning and teaching strategies. Because of this, the teacher also knows they will need to use continuous formative assessment to track this learner, making sure any misconceptions are carefully managed.

Strategies:

- ensuring continuous formative assessment is carried out with this learner as attempts are made to align the intended learning and the actual learning is crucial (CCF 6). Many of the strategies discussed in this chapter can be used to ensure this happens;

- adapting learning and teaching strategies in a responsive way, including targeted support to these specific pupils (CCF 5);

- using high-quality feedback to ensure learners know where they need to further develop, making sure it is clear and accurate information using expert subject knowledge (CCF 6, 3).

UNKNOWN

When in the unknown quadrant neither the teacher nor the learner is aware that they have not learnt the intended learning. It is likely there is confusion and misconceptions may be present in the learner's mind. There are many reasons as to why the teacher may not know that the learner has not achieved the learning. It could be due to instrumental factors, such as not enough time to formatively or summatively assess during or after the lesson. It could be due to gaps in the teacher's subject or curriculum knowledge. Regardless, being in this quadrant means there is a chance that learning will continue to be stifled and unsuccessful. Equally, the teacher is unable to adapt their teaching and learning as they are unaware of the issues that remain.

Example: in the same science lesson a learner has engaged with a learning experience to show they understand the difference between mammals and fish. On this occasion, the learner has developed misconceptions, and the actual learning is not aligned with the intended learning. However, the teacher, due to various factors, is also unaware that this is the case and remains unaware. This could be due to poor or incorrect subject knowledge or not assessing the learner in a timely fashion. As such, neither the learner nor the teacher is aware that the intended and actual learning are incongruent. There is no adaptive strategy put in place and the learner continues to harbour misconceptions in this particular area.

Strategies:

- focusing on different ways to uncover tacit knowledge will be crucial to ensure the teacher can understand what has been learnt so they can adapt their learning and teaching strategies. Looking at patterns of learning over a period of time will also be helpful if anomalies appear in a learner's understanding (CCF 6);

- using expert subject knowledge may be useful to identify where a learner may have developed misconceptions in their understanding (CCF 3);

- beginning teachers should utilise the expertise of their colleagues and avoid assessment pitfalls. This can be through help in planning effective formative assessment activities or informal conversations about learners and what they are demonstrating (CCF 6).

REFLECTIVE ACTIVITY

Using the Johari window model above for assessment, think about your class or a group of learners and a lesson you have recently taught.

Try placing your learners in each of these boxes thinking about a specific lesson or learning outcome you have recently completed.

Based on this, think about the strategies you might use, as discussed above, in the next lesson to ensure you can move your learners into the open box.

FINAL THOUGHTS

Assessment is a complex process and one of the skills we have to develop as a teacher. We have to ensure that we remember that the different kinds of knowledge our learners will need to acquire should be assessed in different ways to ensure success. In primary school teaching, the combination of formative and summative assessment is crucial for a well-rounded approach to student evaluation. However, if we want to continually adapt our learning and teaching strategies to the needs of our learners, we have to ensure that formative assessment remains the major tool we use. Only through formative assessment can we as teachers continually gauge student understanding, identify areas that require additional attention and adapt teaching methods accordingly. Models like the Johari window can help us think about assessment in ways that can enable us to adapt our learning and teaching strategies. This ongoing feedback loop supports a more dynamic and responsive learning environment, fostering a deeper understanding of concepts. Summative assessment, occurring at the end of a unit or academic term, provides a comprehensive overview of students' overall performance but cannot be effective in helping us to adapt teaching responsively in the moment. It helps educators make informed decisions about student progression, provides data for evaluation and offers insights into the effectiveness of pedagogical strategies. However, both formative and summative assessments contribute to a holistic approach to primary education, promoting student success and continuous improvement in teaching practices.

KEY TAKEAWAYS

- Developing a consistent and nuanced assessment practice is a highly skilled craft and one you will develop throughout your time as a teacher. As you develop and grow as a teacher you will be able to incorporate many of the practices and strategies discussed above into your day-to-day work.

- Ensuring your curricular and subject knowledge is as complete as possible will help you to become an expert in what is being learnt in your classroom, not just what you are teaching.

- Remember that the intended learning and actual learning are often not the same thing.

FURTHER READING AND RESOURCE

Mosey, C. and Stothard, J. (2022) Reimagining adaptive teaching: Creating a supportive environment for all learners. *IMPACT: Journal of the Chartered College of Teaching*, 15.

3
GROUPING

━ CHAPTER OBJECTIVES ━

After engaging with this chapter, you will be able to:

- identify the impact that different grouping approaches have upon the classroom environment;
- reflect upon your own philosophy regarding adaptive grouping within your setting;
- experiment with different adaptive approaches, including mixed-attainment grouping.

INTRODUCTION

This chapter will explore the concept of flexible grouping in the classroom as a gateway to adaptive pedagogy. The challenging decisions that must be made by practitioners will be highlighted and suggestions will be offered as to how grouping can support an adaptive classroom, with a particular focus upon opportunities for collaborative work, mixed-attainment grouping and, at the end of this section, ideas that could be implemented practically. Hewitt and Wright (2019) provide a summary of recommendations for empowering learners which includes the importance of knowing your students, knowing the curriculum, together with a range of teaching and learning approaches, and, importantly, being confident in knowing yourself and having trust that you are making the right decisions for your class and its individuals. This is a thread that runs through this chapter; as you read, consider the different environments that you have worked in and reflect upon the way in which groupings have impacted the teaching and learning in that setting.

The motivation to write this chapter is deeply rooted in my personal experiences as a learner (Charlotte). At secondary school, I was placed into a low-attaining maths set; this was the greatest challenge I had faced on my relatively straightforward learning journey, where I had transitioned year on year, making expected progress. In all other areas of the curriculum, I was attaining the standard for my age and was confident and secure in my own ability. I flourished in English and humanities subjects, but struggled to make good progress in maths, despite my best efforts and help from my dad, who became my unofficial tutor. As I progressed into my GCSE years, I continued to experience difficulties in maths and was told that I would be completing the paper that was capped at gaining a grade C, therefore the curriculum that I was taught was also capped – even to this day I have no concept of trigonometry as this was not part of my syllabus and I had no need for the technical scientific calculator that my peers required to solve their demanding equations. You might be thinking that you wish you had not had to go to the trouble of tackling challenging maths, or indeed, like me, you may feel a sense of shame that you were not judged as good enough to attempt aspects of the curriculum that your peers had access to. My self-esteem and confidence were shattered as a teenager; I was frustrated that my potential was limited and the fact that I achieved a high grade on my coursework, which could have elevated my overall award, was not considered. Even into adulthood, I still lack confidence in maths.

THE REQUIREMENT FOR ADAPTION

Government policy establishes clear guidelines linked to adapting teaching, including specific reference within the Ofsted *Education Inspection Framework* (2023a) to differentiation:

> teachers present subject matter clearly, promoting appropriate discussion about the subject matter they are teaching. They check learners' understanding systematically, identify misconceptions accurately and provide clear, direct feedback. In doing so, they respond and adapt their teaching as necessary, without unnecessarily elaborate or differentiated approaches.

Further to this, within Standard 5 of the *Teachers' Standards* (DfE, 2021), 'Adapt teaching to respond to the strengths and needs of all pupils', the following guidance is offered:

- know when and how to differentiate appropriately, using approaches which enable pupils to be taught effectively

- have a secure understanding of how a range of factors can inhibit pupils' ability to learn, and how best to overcome these

- demonstrate an awareness of the physical, social and intellectual development of children, and know how to adapt teaching to support pupils' education at different stages of development

- have a clear understanding of the needs of all pupils, including those with special educational needs; those of high ability; those with English as an additional language; those with disabilities; and be able to use and evaluate distinctive teaching approaches to engage and support them.

(DfE, 2021, pp. 11–12)

There is much research that explores the impact of grouping in classrooms. Historically, it is accepted that flexibility and adaptation is important; however, in reality, approaches including ability grouping underpinned by fixed mindsets are often seen. When visiting beginning teachers whilst on placement, I often enquire about grouping and how the classroom is organ-ised; overwhelmingly the response is that the children are grouped according to their ability and that this is usually fixed. I encourage the beginning teachers to try out different approaches and, despite some feeling that this could be judged as overstepping their responsibility, many take the plunge and experiment with different approaches. One classroom that I visited at the start of the autumn term was arranged in ability groups; the beginning teacher in this class asked if they could try moving the learners into mixed-attainment groups. The outcome was successful and the class teacher decided to continue with the new arrangement, citing benefits including improvements in attainment and perceived self-esteem for the lower-attaining pupils.

Traditionally, differentiation has been implemented as a way to meet the needs of different learners, usually by providing multiple activities pitched at specific levels of attainment around a theme. In both sets of government guidance, the need for adaption is evident; however, the teaching approaches must be explored in more depth – specifically, tackling the issue of how to arrange learners to achieve the optimum learning experience. As prac-titioners, it is imperative that we consider our own philosophies as educators, the resources we have access to (including other adults) and the learners themselves to create the very best environment for effective teaching and learning to take place. According to Taylor et al. (2016), differentiation is more successfully implemented through 'carefully designed, stimu-lating tasks that all students are able to make a start on. This type of task enables the teacher to offer rich feedback to students at all levels of prior attainment to progress' (p. 338). With this in mind, take time to consider the case study below.

CASE STUDY

A school invited me to a staff training event with the intent to reconsider the concept of differentiation and a move towards a more adaptive approach to pedagogy. The leadership team designed a powerful activity to demonstrate the way in which formal differentiation can limit learning potential focusing upon the mathematical concept of tangrams.

Figure 3.1   Tangram

(Continued)

(Continued)

Staff were already arranged in seated table groups, each group was handed an envelope that contained copies of the tangram sheet above, but the activity that was assigned to each group was differentiated. The learning outcome was shared with everyone, 'to explore tangrams'; Table 3.1 shows the activities that took place.

Table 3.1 Activities

Group 1	Colour the tangram sheet and cut out the shapes independently
Group 2	Cut out the shapes and use a pre-populated Venn diagram to sort with a partner
Group 3	Cut out the shapes and create your own criteria to sort the shapes using a blank Venn diagram with your group

Time was given to the adults to complete their tasks; group 1 were busy colouring independently whilst groups 2 and 3 were exploring the shapes in a more collaborative way, group 2 working with a partner and group 3 as a whole-table group. At the end of the activity, the staff were asked how they felt about the task they had undertaken. At first, group 1 said that they enjoyed the colouring in and that they felt relaxed and liked the fact that they were not challenged. However, as groups 2 and 3 explained their learning and shared their Venn diagrams and the rich debates that had taken place as the learners explored the different criteria, group 1 felt like they had not had the same opportunity to develop their understanding and became resentful that they had not been able to explore the tangrams more deeply. Group 2 completed their task quickly using the pre-defined sorting sheet, it was interesting to see their reaction as group 3 were able to talk with confidence about how they had sorted their shapes according to their own criteria; one participant said that they wished they had had the chance to use their own ideas. Although this was just a quick snapshot, the way in which the teachers were put in the position of being a learner was impactful and led to interesting discussions about how differentiation can unwittingly limit a learning experience. What became clear in this scenario was that setting by ability impacts upon expectations and attainment - group 1 had not met the learning outcome of the lesson, this was not because the group did not have the potential to achieve, rather they were not given the opportunity to.

It is important to consider the context for adaptable teaching in our classrooms and, as already suggested, many classrooms still employ a fixed grouping system. The following section will explore attainment grouping in more detail, including why such approaches should be reconsidered when creating an adaptive classroom.

ATTAINMENT GROUPING

In 2006, the Department for Education and Skills (DfES) led research looking into the impact of adapting classroom environments which culminated in a report entitled *Grouping Pupils for Success*. The main findings of this study highlighted the importance of adapting groups to suit the learning objective and an understanding that pupils are not simply homogeneous groups but rather individual learners who should be taught as such, with flexibility and supported by a practitioner who has the tools to be responsive in the moment. Just because a group of children have all achieved the same outcome in a summative assessment, for example, does not mean that they all have the same demands in terms of their learning and required support.

The report shared five takeaways for practitioners to consider:

1. use assessment findings to inform the approach;

2. be flexible and innovative;

3. secure high-quality teaching in all groups;

4. use additional adults effectively;

5. provide pupils with the ability to work in different groupings.

REFLECTIVE ACTIVITY

Although this report was written nearly twenty years ago, do you feel that the five key takeaways above are actioned in contemporary classrooms?

Do you believe that these recommendations are still relevant today? Why? Why not?

Thinking specifically about providing pupils with the ability to work in different groupings, how can this be achieved in your classroom setting? What would you need to consider for this to be successful?

SETTING AND STREAMING

Much research has been conducted over the years to find out what the benefits and limitations of grouping linked to ability are. Blatchford and Webster (2018) explore several issues relating to different classroom contexts across primary and secondary settings and acknowledge that the intention to teach children together in mainstream schools is to be commended; however, it often leads to challenging considerations linked to the organisation of a classroom environment. Historically, the concept of teaching children in set groups has developed from the belief that teaching is more effective when the range of attainment is reduced, but there is limited evidence to support this idea. Grouping by streaming is determined by overall ability, usually across core areas of the curriculum and often observed in secondary settings; this sometimes means that those in the group identified as 'higher' may not be a high attainers across all areas.

The Sutton Trust and Education Endowment Foundation (EEF, 2018b) created teaching and learning toolkits that explore a range of learning approaches including setting and streaming, within class attainment grouping and collaborative learning approaches. The toolkits were created as supportive frameworks and are based on research-informed trials so that schools can explore the ideas presented in their own setting and adapt as required. According to the research, the impact of setting and streaming provides zero months' progress on average, notably with limited outcomes for lower-attaining pupils. Overall, pupils who are taught in streamed or set groups make similar progress to those in mixed-attainment groups; there is a small negative impact on less confident learners and a small positive impact on those who are more secure, which raises the question as to why setting and streaming are such a fundamental part of classroom organisation in schools today. Aligned with the DfES report (2006), the EEF notes that it is very important that the curriculum is challenging but flexible and states that learning should be monitored closely to ensure that activities and expectations are balanced effectively. Interestingly, it also comments upon the wider impact of ability grouping on the whole child, considering self-esteem and self-confidence and the detrimental effect that this can have, manifesting in negative self-fulfilling prophecies. Learners who are grouped with others who struggle are cited as being affected by subconscious bias and are more likely to be taught by less experienced staff.

In contrast to the experiences of those in lower-attaining groups, Boaler (1997) evaluated the experiences of higher attainers and found that the anxiety and stress that is experienced by some pupils in these high-pressured environments can be debilitating. One child interviewed for the research paper reflected upon the pace of lessons and confided that they were often confused, particularly in maths lessons, where it was a regular occurrence that they were using a method of calculation without really having a depth of understanding linked to what the method meant or when it should be applied appropriately. Boaler (1997) argues that 'although setting is thought to push higher attainers to even higher peaks of attainment' (p.166), the negative outcome for some learners is beyond an academic impact.

▬ REFLECTIVE ACTIVITY ▬

After reading this summary about setting and streaming, what does your experience tell you about the approach?

Can you think of children that you have taught in a similar context who may have been impacted either positively or negatively by setting and streaming?

WITHIN CLASS ATTAINMENT GROUPING

Similar to setting and despite the debate as to its effectiveness, within-class ability grouping is predominantly implemented as a way of organising learners in primary schools, where tables of children with similar attainment are seated together, often completing differentiated activities like the example in the reflective activity at the start of this chapter. In this type of grouping, learners are given the same curriculum diet, but tasks are varied to suit the needs of the children. The EEF (2018b) states that this type of grouping, often known as attainment grouping, demonstrates a positive impact on progress, on average two months; however, this has a caveat that the evidence is limited in support of this claim and, interestingly, the impact on progress in English was not as evident as that of maths. This approach to grouping provides a greater degree of flexibility in terms of organisation and adaptation; along with careful monitoring, learners can move into different groups depending on their confidence and attainment in a particular lesson. As discussed in Chapter 6, Adaptive interventions, grouping in this way can allow learners to have targeted support from the teacher or teaching assistant following on from formative assessment. However, it could be argued that all too often children are fixed within a group and that their potential to thrive and progress is stifled by teacher expectation. Such groupings can lead to issues around self-confidence and self-esteem, regardless of age; children are aware of individual abilities of their peers and labelling should be treated with the utmost caution. The practice of naming tables according to ability is something that is particularly interesting. When visiting a classroom, your perception of the children seated on the dodecahedron table would probably be different to those seated on the triangle table, for example.

MIS-GROUPING

Mis-grouping is regarded as one of the main challenges linked to attainment grouping of learners and a number of reports highlight this concern. Effective assessment processes should run as a thread throughout all adaptive practice and classroom management; mis-grouping is a by-product of teachers not knowing their students adequately and, more concerningly, having varying expectations, set assumptions and a fixed perception of the learners in their class. Research conducted by the Department for Children, Schools and Families (DfCSF) (Dyson et al., 2007) identified how social status can lead to mis-grouping of children – with those identified as having a lower social-economic status being more likely to be placed in a lower-attaining group, in contrast to their higher-status social-economic peers who were assigned to a higher-attaining group. The same was seen for minority ethnic groups and SEND children, who were more likely to be placed in a group with lower expectations. Mis-grouping can lead to significant issues including learners becoming disaffected and frustrated; the perception of a child who is placed in the wrong group can have a detrimental effect on their future, with individuals becoming disaffected and demoralised by their education, sometimes resulting in challenging behaviours, suspension and exclusion. Headline figures from *Suspensions and Permanent Exclusions in England: Autumn Term 2022/3* (DfE, 2023b) reveal that the suspension rate for children eligible for free school meals (FSM) is more than four times that for non-FSM eligible children, the rate of suspensions for children identified as SEN without an EHCP is 8.16 per cent, this compares to 1.94 per cent for pupils with no SEN. Although it would be foolish to attribute these statistics solely to mis-grouping of children, the stark facts and figures presented here should surely not be overlooked.

REFLECTIVE ACTIVITY

Can you think about a learner who has been mis-grouped in a particular setting in which you have taught?

As a Beginning teacher it can be challenging to raise a concern such as mis-grouping to your mentor, but you have a professional responsibility to follow this up.

What steps could you take to manage such a situation?

INCLUSIVE AND ADAPTIVE GROUPING

MIXED-ATTAINMENT GROUPING

Mixed-attainment grouping (sometimes referred to as heterogeneous grouping) is achieved by organising groups beyond academic attainment. For example, a group could be created by considering friendship groups or personal characteristics or simply created randomly. Teachers should know their learners and be able to allocate groupings based on their knowledge of the individual. For example, one child may be confident in an aspect of the curriculum but lack confidence in their own ability; they could be grouped with another learner who is less confident academically but is able to support and reassure their peers, together with third child who has similar personal interests to the other two children. These groups should not be fixed; instead, they should be regularly reallocated so that the learners can work with others and build relationships with their classmates. This kind of grouping takes time to establish effectively; the learners need support to work well together and the teacher must model this carefully. Creating a classroom environment based upon mixed-ability grouping is seen as challenging. Indeed, Taylor et al. (2016) acknowledged that most data they collected linked to their investigations into mixed-ability grouping demonstrated a reluctance to try the approach and that a 'nature of fear' was evident in many schools (p. 341).

Despite the challenge of the unknown for many teachers, when enacted well, mixed-attainment grouping helps to promote self-esteem and positive attitudes to learning. Hallam and Ireson (2006) found that lower attainers and disadvantaged learners in secondary school settings are more likely to prefer this type of grouping, although some pupils did state that they preferred being in their own attainment set as they sometimes felt a little overwhelmed with new learning. This could be overcome with the provision of scaffolded support and specific resources; however, it is important to be aware of this challenge.

The EEF's project *Best Practice in Mixed Attainment Grouping* (2018a) struggled to recruit schools; out of 158 that were invited to participate, only eighteen signed up to the pilot which reaffirms how cautious and reluctant schools can be towards the approach. According to the findings, teachers had mixed feelings about enacting mixed-attainment groups, although those settings that continued to follow the approach believed that the lower attainers benefited the most overall. It was recognised that a good level of training is arranged for staff and that communicating high expectations for all learners is essential, 'if mixed-attainment practice is to be widely adopted, a supportive policy climate will need to be created' (p. 341). Returning to the five recommendations of the DfES (2006), if a practitioner uses assessment to inform an approach, is flexible and innovative, is secure in delivering high-quality teaching, uses additional adults effectively and can provide pupils with the ability to work in different groupings, creating a mixed-attainment classroom should be achievable.

The following ideas could be implemented as part of a mixed-attainment classroom; however, it is important to be aware that each of these grouping solutions do have their challenges and cannot be implemented instantly. They would require modelling and, in some cases, training to secure the best outcomes for the learners. Every learner and learning environment is unique; however, these ideas will provide some approaches for you to adapt for your classroom setting.

GROUP WORK/COLLABORATIVE GROUPING

Group work occurs when learners work together cooperatively to achieve the same learning outcome and, according to Baines et al. (2008), 'Its inclusive nature is likely to encourage higher levels of participation and engagement for every child in the class' (p. 8). Within a classroom environment, children often sit together in groups, but if you reflect upon what this looks like in reality, the chances are that purposeful interactions and opportunities for working together are, in fact, quite limited – often because the task set may not be suited to group work or that the teacher has not supported the approach sufficiently with modelling or monitoring so that purposeful collaboration can take place.

The Training and Development Agency for Schools (TDA) (2008) highlighted key features that underpin effective collaborative group work:

- the group has a shared goal;

- individual pupils are given complementary and specific roles, such as scribe, timekeeper, chairperson and so on. These roles can be tailored to the capacity of the members of the group;

- everyone relies on the others for the task to be completed;

- group members work together over a period of time and establish a group identity;

- pupils are taught the necessary skills for effective group functioning;

- pupils are given opportunities to consider how well they work together and what improvements can be made to the way they function.

Firstly, the classroom environment needs to be conducive to group working; furniture should be arranged so that it is a communication-friendly space. Having children seated in rows has been shown to reduce challenging behaviour in classes; however, a significant limitation is that this kind of layout inhibits purposeful interaction between learners. Baines et al. (2008) and the EEF (2018b) explore grouping sizes in some detail. Pairs and threes enable a good level of discussion, similar to that of peer tutoring which will be discussed later; however, there is a risk with an odd number that someone will be left out. Small groups of four to six learners can be effective for planning around an idea or for reflection on opinions, although there is the potential for some children to feel overwhelmed and they may fade into the background of the discussion. On balance, three to five learners in a group provides an effective balance in most cases, where the group is small enough to give everyone the opportunity to play their part and contribute. It is vital for the facilitator of group work to balance learners' needs carefully; when managed well, learners will develop their social and communication skills and will be able to offer a level of challenge but also, importantly, an opportunity to support to their peers and this would be achieved through mixed-attainment grouping. A more knowledgeable adult is often recognised as the person who helps a learner move through the Zone of Proximal Development (ZPD), as stated by Vygotsky (1978); however, this role is not limited to adults – peers can also enact this role.

Collaborative group work brings a number of benefits which are highlighted in the EEF (2018b) toolkit; interestingly, their research found that the impact of learners working together collaboratively on a task makes an additional five months' progress on average over the course of the academic year, which is an impressive claim.

▬ CASE STUDY ▬

Mr Park has researched about the benefits of problem-based learning as part of his initial teacher training course. He wants to offer a different approach to the traditional teaching style of telling the learners what they need to know and is keen to develop a sequence of learning based on problem-based, real-life approaches. In English, the children have been working for three weeks on writing persuasive texts; this has included looking at examples, paired writes, modelled writes, supported by scaffolded activities including vocabulary mats and a working wall in the classroom. The focus for the learners to explore in this activity is the threat of a housing redevelopment on the school field.

In groups, children are assigned the problem by Mr Park, and, as facilitator, he guides them through the issue. However, the emphasis is that the learners are at the centre of this real-world problem. In small mixed-attainment groups, the children define the problem and identify steps to present their case and, together, write their letters. Finally, the letters are shared with the headteacher and the governing body of the school.

Before collaborative group work can be established in a setting, it is important to set the boundaries and share a collective vision for how the approach works in practice. Learners can contribute to this framework which must include reference to communication skills – for example, negotiation, empathy, active listening and, of course, patience. For collaborative group work to be effective, the approach must be embedded into the classroom environment; when the firm foundations are laid, opportunities for improved communication, creativity and critical thinking will naturally evolve.

PEER TUTORING

Peer tutoring encompasses a range of pedagogical approaches where learners can work together with a partner to support each other in several ways; this can be fixed-role tutoring with a more knowledgeable other, or reciprocal, where the role of tutor and tutee may change depending on the task. As with collaborative grouping, peer tutoring is an approach which can support self-esteem and confidence; however, there are limitations and, as with all pedagogical approaches that a teacher may have in their toolkit, it is important to monitor and have a good understanding of the needs of all learners. The EEF (2018b) suggests that it is those learners who lack confidence and are less secure in their learning and SEND learners that make the most progress when participating in peer tutoring and that confidence and motivation is boosted; however, Roberts (2016) notes that it could undermine self-confidence and that it is important to create a partnership centred around being 'a co-collaborator rather than a teacher of those less capable' (p. 44).

Peer tutoring requires careful management; before it can become part of the daily routine in a learning environment, careful modelling and training is required. Again, like the collaborative group work approach, children could sign up to a framework of guidance or help to create their own list of boundaries to ensure consistency of approach. Resources are required to support the learning activities; this could include key questions to be asked, scaffolding guides etc. According to the EEF (2018b), peer tutoring is most effective when scheduled regularly; it suggests that four- to ten-week blocks with four to five regular sessions a week have most impact.

Roberts (2016) recorded observations between two children, one confident learner and another who was less secure in their understanding; the article provides an interesting insight into peer tutoring and the impact that the interactions had on both learners. Although it could be assumed that the partnership was mainly arranged to the benefit of the child with less confidence, the impact to both learners exceeded initial expectations. As a practitioner, Roberts was becoming more frustrated with the 'obsession' of providing sufficient challenge for students identified as 'high achievers' through quantity over quality; for her, using the learners themselves as resources to 'develop a pedagogy that enables all learners to flourish' was the driving force (p. 51). The reciprocal benefits of paired tutoring went beyond an academic focus, although the opportunity for revisiting past learning was seen to benefit all learners. Roberts noted that the more secure learner, in her observations, often lacked confidence and courage; working with their peer supported them to be more assertive. By varying expectations and assumptions, moving away from the norm and a fixed-mindset way of grouping and permitting interactions between learners, the classroom was re-energised and revitalised.

SNOWBALLING

Snowballing is a collaborative group approach that could be implemented as part of an adaptive classroom and incorporates the benefits of both group work and paired work as outlined previously. In this scenario, the teacher, Mr Davies, has grouped his Year 6 class in a mixed-attainment seating arrangement; the children are used to working with each other as part of their classroom routine. For their design and technology (DT) project, the pupils have been looking at structures and electrical circuits. Mr Davies has given the class a challenge to design a fairground ride that moves in a circular motion. The following steps would be followed as part of the snowballing approach; this would be over a sequence of lessons and the steps could be easily adapted for any problem-solving activity across the curriculum.

CASE STUDY

Step 1: In the whole-class teaching input, Mr Davies revisits the learning that has already taken place in this DT topic, recapping on the electrical circuits that have been made in previous lessons; the children would have the opportunity to look back through their completed work and reflect on their journey so far.

Step 2: Mr Davies provides a range of images showing fairground rides that move in a circular motion. Websites are shared for the children to access to explore rides in more detail, including those at the local amusement park that the children visited recently on their school trip to support learning during this topic.

Step 3: Independently, the children access resources provided by Mr Davies. Based on knowledge of the learners, he supports pupils who may need extra support and circulates the classroom, providing guidance if required. Mr Cashmore, the class teaching assistant, is also on hand should anyone need additional help.

Step 4: The children make notes and record any key information that they may find useful when planning. Mr Davies models this as a whole-class input and time is allocated in the session so that talking partners are able to share and reflect upon their ideas. Observation and discussion with learners allows both Mr Davies and Mr Cashmore to gain an understanding of how the learners are progressing and whether they require extra support. The mixed-attainment groupings mean that expertise is balanced around the room and that the conversations on the tables will promote and encourage the sharing of ideas.

Step 5: Mr Davies provides a modelled example of the drawing of a simple rotary fairground ride and shares a scaffolding list of non-negotiables with the children, including requirements of a name, theme, working rotary motion etc. The children begin to plan their idea and annotate their drawings, including making a list of resources that will be needed.

Step 6: Mr Davies shares key questions to consider on the board, such as: what is the theme of your fairground ride? Who is the target audience for your ride? What do you think will be the most challenging thing to construct? Are you unsure about how to create part of your design – can you help your partner to think this through? Again, talking partners share their ideas and are encouraged to act as critical friends; the questions given by Mr Davies help to structure this support.

Step 6: The talking partners then join with another set of talking partners so that they can share their ideas together. The key questions provide ongoing support in this larger group of four. The groups are carefully arranged so that if there are any learners who are unsure of the task or limited on ideas, they are grouped with children who are more confident with their learning.

Step 7: In a whole-class group, the children are now able to share their ideas to the rest of their peers; this is achieved in a gallery approach, the designs are presented around the room, the children are on hand to answer any questions about their work. Post-it notes are fixed onto work by peers with constructive comments linked to the key questions from the start of the design process, including comments linked to feasibility. The children are familiar with the 'gallery' and have experience of the benefits of receiving and giving (constructive) feedback.

Step 8: The children are now able to continue the sequence of this lesson with the construction of their fairground ride; this will be followed up with talking partners evaluating the final outcomes of the project.

This scenario was based on an observation from a Year 6 classroom; however, the snowball approach could be used with learners of all ages and, as with all of these ideas, could be easily adapted to suit the needs of any pupils, regardless of age or level of confidence. By implementing adaptive and interactive pedagogies such as this into a classroom routine, the richer and more vibrant the environment will become.

THINK, PAIR, SHARE

As part of an adaptive teaching toolkit, *think, pair, share* is easy to use as a supportive strategy in the moment and can help to build the confidence of learners. This does not need to be pre-planned or formally arranged; pupils can be paired strategically or randomly depending on the circumstances. The following case study gives an example of how this strategy can be employed.

CASE STUDY

Miss Akanbi shared the following word problem with her class of Year 3 children during the whole-class input section of her maths lesson. *Altogether in the school library there are 120 books all about animals and countries. There are 82 books on animals on the top shelf, how many books about countries are on the bottom shelf?*

First, Miss Akanbi asked the children to *think* for 30 seconds about how they might solve this problem. The children had whiteboards to jot down ideas if they wanted to.

After 30 seconds, the children turned to their *pair* – in this scenario the children had allocated talking partners sitting next to them on their mixed-attainment group table – and discussed their thoughts.

Finally, Miss Akanbi asked the pairs to *share* their ideas as to how they would solve the problem.

In this scenario, support was structured so that those learners who may not have been confident in being able to start to solve the problem would be supported by a partner who may have been able to strategise to find a solution. Of course, the challenge could be if both learners were struggling; in this case Miss Akanbi would be assessing understanding by observing interactions and stepping in if required. Tailoring the next part of the lesson so that the learners could be supported in a focused group could be a solution, as explored in Chapter 6, Adaptive intervention. Careful modelling of the steps to reach the answer after sharing would also provide more support; scaffolding learning with another example in a similar style could be helpful here. The benefit of think, pair, share is that there is no pressure on learners to perform in front of their peers; a limitation could be that a higher-attaining child could just 'feed' an answer to their partner and this could lead to a masking of misunderstanding and a widening gap between learners. Pupils should be coached in using the approach so that this can be minimised; steps to success and breaking down learning can help to overcome this.

JIGSAW GROUPING

This grouping approach is particularly effective when used to research and present work collaboratively, giving all learners a responsibility to contribute to their group's final piece of work.

═══ **CASE STUDY** ═══

Mr Woodbury has challenged his mixed Year 4 and 5 class to create a poster to illustrate their geography topic looking at rainforests – specifically, why they are under threat and why this is such a problem for the world. This is the fourth session in a sequence of lessons. The class has already explored what rainforests are and where they are located; they have visited both the local and school libraries and created a book corner of resources all about the rainforests. The children have also been signposted to online resources to support their developing knowledge. Mr Woodbury arranges his class into mixed-attainment groupings of four learners per group. For this activity, he has identified four key areas to research: why the rainforests are important; why are the rainforests under threat; which species are endangered; and how deforestation can affect humans throughout the world. Each child will choose an area to research, as the expert in this 'field'; the learners will leave their 'home' group and move to a group in which the children are researching the same topic. This allows for greater socialisation and collaboration between peers; adaptive support can be offered as required by the teacher. Scaffolding can also be provided with some key questioning or word mats for the children to access. It is the intention that the children will work together as experts to develop their knowledge on their theme.

When the research is completed, the children can then return to their home group with their research and the original group can then build this into their poster. Each child starts off as an expert in one area of knowledge, but helps to create a piece of group work that includes research over four key areas. In this type of approach, there is a sense of responsibility for the group as each person is accountable for their own research and dissemination. The role of the teacher is pivotal in this scenario; monitoring is essential to check that everyone can access the task and contribute effectively.

═══ **REFLECTIVE ACTIVITY** ═══

Think about an opportunity within a teaching and learning sequence where you could implement a jigsaw approach or reflect on a sequence that you have already taught, but would provide an opportunity for this type of grouping to be used.

How would you ensure that the task is adapted to suit the needs of all learners? What scaffolding support would you put in place to ensure success for all?

What would be the challenges that this approach could bring?

Think about social interactions, expectations for behaviour and co-operation, active listening etc.

How could you manage these elements to create a successful, collaborative classroom environment?

EXPERT OTHER

Expert other is a supportive approach that can be implemented very quickly and fits in well with the other ideas shared in this section. Often, when a misconception arises in the classroom, it can be a barrier for more than one learner. The following case study illustrates how collaborative working can help to overcome misconceptions.

CASE STUDY

Miss Brown was 'marking in the moment' during a maths lesson with her Year 1 class. The children were learning how to apply the symbols of greater than, less than and equal to (<,>,=) and, as she marked Issy's work, Miss Brown noticed that she had confused the symbols. Miss Brown responded by spending time supporting Issy with further examples. She gave her copies of crocodile mouth visual resources that had been used in the main input of the lesson as a scaffold; this helped Issy to visualise the symbols more confidently and, when the teacher was happy that Issy was more secure with her understanding, she left Issy to work independently. When Miss Brown continued to mark other learners' work, she noticed that Marcus had also become confused with the symbols. This time, she asked Issy to be the 'expert other' and support her peer. As Issy gave advice, Miss Brown observed and was ready to intervene to ensure that the correct guidance was being given. As a learner, Issy felt empowered that she was able to support a peer with a concept that, at first, she had found challenging. Such collaborative approaches promote a sense of collegiality in the classroom and have the potential to boost the self-esteem of those learners who may often feel overwhelmed. Expert others must be managed carefully so that the message is consistent and correct, but they can quickly become a foundation of successful mixed-attainment grouping.

FINAL THOUGHTS

Above all, this chapter aims to encourage self-reflection and critical thinking about what is being offered to the learners in your class and how little changes to pedagogy and grouping could make a significant difference to the self-esteem and, in some cases, attainment of pupils. What is clear is that – regardless of grouping, scaffolding and interventions – quality teaching from the outset is what provides the firmest of foundations; from this the possibilities can be endless. Florian and Black-Hawkins (2011) outline key recommendations that can be taken and used to underpin a community classroom in which all learners are able to make progress together:

- creating learning opportunities that are sufficiently made available for everyone, so that all learners are able to participate in classroom life;

- extending what is ordinarily available for all learners (creating a rich community) rather than using teaching and learning strategies that are suitable for most alongside something additional or different for some who experience difficulties;

- focusing on what is to be taught (and how) rather than who is to learn it;

- rejecting deterministic beliefs about ability being fixed and the associated idea that the presence of some will hold back the progress of others;

- believing all children will make progress, learn and achieve;

- focusing teaching and learning on what children can do rather than what they cannot do;

- using a variety of grouping strategies to support everyone's learning rather than relying on ability grouping to separate (able from less able students);

- using formative assessment to support learning;

- seeing difficulties in learning as a professional challenge rather than a deficit in learners and encouraging new ways of working;

- seeking and trying out new ways of working to support the learning of all children;

- working with and through other adults that respect the dignity of learners as full members of the community of the classroom;

- being committed to CPD as a way of developing more inclusive practices.

(Adapted from Florian and Black-Hawkins, 2011, pp. 813–28)

REFLECTIVE ACTIVITY

Thinking about your current classroom setting, reflect upon how you could embed one or more of the approaches discussed in this chapter into your practice.

What are the challenges of implementing the approaches? These could be specific to the needs of the learners in the class and could go beyond academic needs – for example, how could a learner with behavioural needs be supported to engage? If you have additional language learners, how could these approaches support their needs? Remember that such approaches could indeed provide a greater level of assistance for these learners.

How could you 'sell' these approaches to colleagues and change mindsets when many practitioners are fearful of mixed-attainment groupings?

— KEY TAKEAWAYS ————————————————————

- Effective adaptive grouping is not something that can be achieved instantly, it takes time to build the skills associated with many of these pedagogical approaches; however, the benefits academically, socially and emotionally are worth your effort.

- As a beginning teacher it is natural to feel overwhelmed and sense a lack of sufficient authority to make a change within a classroom that is not necessarily yours. As Florian and Black-Hawkins (2011) assert, seeking new solutions are part of the professional challenge; be brave and make the change – if you know your learners well, the benefits will soon become clear.

FURTHER READING AND RESOURCES

Coe. R (2014) *The Politics of Setting.*
https://giftedphoenix.wordpress.com/2014/11/12/the-politics-of-setting/

The Bell Foundation
bell-foundation.org.uk/resources/

4

ADAPTABLE ENVIRONMENTS AND EXPERIENCES

┌───┐

━ CHAPTER OBJECTIVES ━

After engaging with this chapter, you will be able to:

*   understand what an adaptive learning environment looks and feels like;
*   recognise how to make your learning environment more adaptive;
*   recognise how to create adaptive and accessible learning experiences.

└───┘

INTRODUCTION

Let us begin with a simple and common analogy. Take a seed which you want to germinate and grow. You plant the seed and watch it over time, but nothing happens. You ask yourself why this is the case, what have I done wrong? Of course, you can think that there is something wrong with the seed you have planted, but, likely, the seed does not have the right conditions to germinate and grown. Simply, the environment in which the seed is planted is not conducive to its growth and potential. This simple change of thinking is extremely helpful when considering the environment, which may be a classroom, in which learners are taught.

Teaching and learning can be related to this analogy. School should be an environment that is safe and stimulating for all learners, but this is not always the case. Not all children find school and its environment to be spaces in which they can thrive and grow. Sadly, because of this, many children feel they are not made for learning or, even worse, think they are failures at learning. As teachers, senior leaders and stakeholders in education we are all working together for a common purpose: to help individuals learn and grow in our learning environments. If we reflect, many teaching initiatives and educational practices are focused on trying to change and do something to the learner, that there is something wrong with the learner to begin with that needs remedying. We attempt to give and impart information to children, in an act of teaching. We offer them activities to complete so we can impart our knowledge to them and assess what they have learnt. We remove children from classrooms or separate them from other learners in the form of intervention, suggesting that it is the seed that is problematic rather than the environment. This is because we often focus so heavily on teaching, we forget that children learn regardless of us. Much of what we have focused on here is about teaching, but we must remember that children naturally learn. Of course, we are not arguing that learners do not need different things to develop and grow – exactly the opposite. It is likely that in our learning and teaching repertoire we may use strategies which seem exclusionary, but we are advocating for a shift in culture here. If we get the environment right, our learners will naturally flourish in spite of what we teach.

Equally, we take the opposite route and focus merely on ourselves as teachers as the problem. This can also be challenging. If we return to the analogy of the seed, we can consider ourselves as a gardener. We can provide the best environment for a seed, but without an essential component, such as carbon dioxide, it is likely the seed will not grow and survive – if it germinates at all. However, we can begin to judge our own abilities as a gardener, overly focusing on our own actions should a seed not germinate, when actually we need to think more holistically about the wider environment and the effect this has on a seed. As teachers, we are experts in knowing our learners and, more importantly, how they learn. We recognise, with experience and confidence, that if one of the conditions is not present, no matter how amazing our teaching is, our learners will not develop.

Consider a time when you bought a plant and placed it in a spot in your home. It seems to get less and less healthy, so you move it to a different spot in which it flourishes. The plant appears to grow without any interaction or interference from yourself. This is what we hope to achieve when creating an accessible and adaptive learning environment. A learning space where our learners thrive with only minimal interference from us. This chapter will help us to think differently about learning and teaching and how the environment we create can have a huge impact on the culture of learning in our school. This is not an easy process and makes us step outside our comfort zone, but we encourage and urge you to think deeply about this. Many may argue that, just as there is an infinite number of seeds which require different environments, there are huge numbers of children each of whom need different conditions to thrive. Indeed, but, just like seeds, if we think carefully there are commonalities across these conditions that are conducive to all learners, which allow all children to learn.

REFLECTIVE ACTIVITY

The above analogy was given in an attempt to make clear how important school environments are and how they can provide successful spaces for learning. We can, as teachers, begin reflecting on how effective we feel these spaces are for our learners. We can begin this reflective process by considering the following questions.

Do you assume that all children think and learn in the same way?

Do you believe that learning and thinking is a fixed process?

Can you think of a time a learner in your class has flourished because of your learning environment? What factors or conditions made this happen?

After reflecting upon and answering these questions, perhaps engage in a professional discussion with a colleague to get their opinions and thoughts on this. Do they think differently or similarly to you on this topic?

DIFFERENTIATION AND LEARNING EXPERIENCES

It is important, at this point, to relate some of what we have been talking about to the concept of *differentiation*. Much has already been written about how to differentiate activities for different learners in the classroom. The seminal author Tomlinson (2014) wrote extensively in many texts about the practice of differentiation, albeit from an American context aimed at a wider international audience. This has formed a lot of practice which has aimed at making pedagogy, curriculum and assessment appropriate for learners of different ages and educational stages. Whilst it is clear that differentiation and adaptive teaching are connected in some respects, we argue they are not the same thing and that there are some key differences between these approaches. On two levels, we suggest differentiation and adaptive teaching are quite different – the first being the mindset which underpins each of these approaches; the second being at an instrumental level, the level of practice in schools.

With regard to mindset, it is clear that there has been much change in our approach to helping learners achieve through creating a learning environment and learning experiences. A reading of Tomlinson (2014) suggests that teachers should often try to individualise their approaches to learning and teaching to make their pedagogic and assessment strategies as appropriate as possible to a diverse community of learners. However, as the DfE states in the ECF (2019a), there must be a recognition that such practices can have an adverse effect on the ways in which teachers think about learning, reducing their expectations of some learners and raising their expectations of others. This is an example of a 'lethal mutation' (as discussed in Chapter 1, Introduction), which involves taking a practice and modifying it to a specific context which renders it no longer as effective, or even become detrimental. Essentially, differentiation had the adverse effect of producing in the minds of teachers a view that some learners can achieve whilst others cannot.

With regard to instrumental practice, there are a few differences to note. Tomlinson (2014) argued that one might differentiate by content, process, product and environment. These different ways of differentiating based on learners' needs seemed an excellent way of making sure that the individual needs of learners were catered for, through an increasingly individualised approach to learning and teaching. However, there were unforeseen consequences of this approach which were detrimental to learning and teaching in classroom. As many teachers came to realise, the process of differentiating became a time-consuming and difficult task, attempting to meet the individual needs of each learner with a specific and unique task. It also became clear that as teachers attempted to differentiate content for individuals, different groups of learners were accessing a completely different curriculum to their peers. Not only this, but different groups of learners were accessing varying degrees of pedagogic quality, with some learners being removed from learning environments for more specialised forms of teaching. Thus, over time, different groups of learners were receiving a completely different quality of education in our classrooms. Whilst this was certainly not the intention of Tomlinson, it was, nevertheless, an outcome. Many of the ideas discussed above were also explored in a four-year longitudinal study by Boaler et al. (2000). Equally, the DfE's (2019a, p. 17) ECF states that adaptive teaching will not be as effective if it 'causes teachers to artificially create distinct tasks for different groups of pupils or to set lower expectations for particular pupils'. Thus, a shift of practice is needed away from antiquated methods which perpetuate because 'that's how we have always done these things'. Whilst much research shows there is little personal or academic benefit to differentiating based on ability, this practice is still common in schools.

SEYMOUR PAPERT: CENTRAL LOGO DESIGN

It is clear that as time develops our classrooms and learning environments are becoming more diverse and the interests, experiences and needs of our learners are gradually increasing. Whilst all learners share the same basic needs, such as to feel safe and happy, there is much about our learners that is different. We are asked to disaggregate our learners from being a large mass into individuals, thinking about them less as a group and more as individual people. However, as teachers we recognise it is time-consuming and challenging to teach individually to every learner in our classrooms. The DfE's (2021) *Teachers' Standards* state we must have an awareness of various factors affecting our students' physical, social and intellectual development, as well as how we should adapt our teaching to these developing needs at different times and stages. Equally, creating a learning environment in which our learners feel safe and stimulated is crucial. Thus, to begin rethinking our learning environments, to make them as accessible and adaptive as possible, it is important that we have a model to help us do this. Using models and other ideas can help us step outside our comfort zone or everyday ways of thinking about education. One such model is that suggested by Seymour Papert (1980) in his book *Mindstorms: Children, Computers and Powerful Ideas*. His model, whilst used in the context of teaching computing and mathematics, has direct implications for general educational thought and practice. Below we shall discuss some of the keys features of his model and how they might translate to your own learning environments. Whilst picking and choosing what we like about these ideas might be a good starting point, it is also useful to think about these learning environments in a holistic way. If we want to develop and change our learning practices and environments, we have to change our thinking and culture too. It cannot just be a tokenistic effort.

LOGO DESIGN PRINCIPLES

Papert suggested an educational model called the Central Logo Design, which contains some interesting features which can be applied to any learning environment and is perfectly suited to a primary school classroom. Many of these features focus on holistic ways in which to develop and create a learning environment in which learners can learn and progress. An important distinction in these learning environments, and one that will be explored in greater detail, is the difference between the teacher as an *instructor* (expert) and as an *interventionist* (learner). Traditional and behaviouristic ways of understanding education and learning still exist and often position the teacher as an expert who must impart their knowledge to their pupils through transmission. As time has passed, this model has become seen as increasingly outdated and inaccessible, not to mention fixed rather than adaptive. Situating the teacher as an interventionist means they focus on creating an environment which facilitates learning, rather than directly teaching. Of course, interventionist teachers are still utilising highly effective practice such as explicit modelling, which is research-informed and evidence-based. Many of these features, discussed below, may be well-known to you as a practitioner, however some may not. We have condensed these features into particular categories to signify their main aspects, but we acknowledge they may and should overlap into others.

RELATIONSHIPS

Accessible and adaptable learning environments are:

- rich in human relationships which are actively fostered and developed;

- prioritise relationships with all learners in a classroom, not only peer groups.

CULTURE

Accessible and adaptable learning environments create a culture where:

- cultural sensitivity and the needs of the community are paramount. Individuals are treated with dignity and respect as humans and learners;

- teachers are interventionists, not instructors; they ask questions, provide support, demonstrate and model recognising that students learn, regardless of teachers;

- the flow of ideas, knowledge and instruction is not a one-way street, but a collaboration between the community of learning in a classroom;

- because knowledge and ideas are varied, diversity is celebrated and encouraged;

- learners focus on debugging and not on mistakes, recognising that making errors is an essential aspect of learning, not an inconvenience along the way.

ACTIVITY

Within these learning environments, you will find:

- that learning is a real (not fabricated) activity which is shared by all community members, not just 'students';

- that the activity is extremely varied and discovery-rich, rather than simply worksheets or common tasks that are repeated every day in a similar way;

- learning experiences are designed to foster deep and rich interactions rather than instrumental products at the end of the activity;

- that modifying and adapting work happens in relation to other learners in the environment, based on their varying experiences and expertise as learners;

- that although learners may work independently, they speak to one another and engage.

These features, whilst slightly abstract here, will be discussed in more depth in the next section.

CREATING AN ADAPTIVE LEARNING ENVIRONMENT IN PRACTICE

Creating an accessible and adaptive learning environment may sound easy to some and challenging to others. We argue that it is more than simply changing the layout of a classroom, simply adapting an activity or using different language. It is a shift of thinking and practice: simply put, a change of culture in our classrooms. Whilst Papert's work is relatively unknown, some of his ideas have begun to be introduced to the educational field. One such way is in mathematics, where it has been implemented as a pedagogical strategy for teaching alongside a mastery approach. The Central Logo Design has been explored in forms such as low-threshold, high-ceiling tasks – now a common concept in mathematics teaching and learning, but less commonly used as a pedagogical culture. To exemplify this point, consider these two learning environments and consider which you would prefer to learn in. Whilst some aspects of each environment may be positive, think about which environment is more conducive to learning.

Classroom One:

The learners are writing a report of a fictitious event. Learners sit quietly and are listening to the teacher who is standing at the front of the classroom. The teacher models good practice of how to plan a report, sharing essential criteria which are written on a board. Learners offer suggestions and ideas which are received well. Some are included but some are not because they do not fit the remit of the task. Learners sit in groups which are designed based on their perceived ability in writing. Soon the learners move on to completing a task on their table. Beautiful worksheets are presented, and they are differentiated based on their ability. It contains learning criteria and individual learners know what they are working towards. Some learners struggle with the activity they have been assigned whilst others move through it with ease. After some time, it is clear that the activity is too difficult for some and too easy for others. Over time, learners become slightly disengaged and require motivation to keep up with the task.

Classroom Two:

The learners are writing a report for their local newspaper about an event that took place in their school. They know it will be typed up, printed and sent to other children and adults at home. They talk and discuss what will be needed in their newspaper report and the children share a range of ideas. Vocabulary, content, structure, images and quality are all discussed. The teacher sits alongside a group of learners, discussing ideas with them and making suggestions about how they can improve their work. They use a range of materials on their desk to exemplify their thinking and ideas before moving to another table to discuss with a new group of learners. The teacher discusses the interests of their learners, referring to individual experiences. Discussion is ongoing and the learners make notes and discuss with others. It isn't long before learners are encouraged to move around the environment, looking at different prompts and speaking to other learners. Critical learning moments take place in which the exchange of ideas means some learners take a different viewpoint on the article or are inspired to include different elements in their plans. Learners help one another, also exploring opportunities to improve their work and pointing out anomalies and misconceptions in others' notes. The teacher stops the activity at intervals, sometimes to offer expert advice, model something or simply to demonstrate good examples that others may learn from. Learners seem engaged.

▬ REFLECTIVE ACTIVITY ▬

Looking at the two classroom learning environments above. Consider the following.

- Which of these two learning environments would you prefer to work in?
- Explore and explain why that is. What are the features that stand out to you as being more beneficial to your individual learning preferences?
- What advice would you give to further improve these two learning spaces?

CREATING AN ADAPTIVE AND ACCESSIBLE LEARNING ENVIRONMENT

No matter how good a learning activity may be, or how successfully a leadership team might have embedded the Logo Central Design theory into their school, if teachers do not change their way of thinking, there will be little success of changing the learning culture of the classroom. Many people know that tokenistic approaches to changing education practices without a change in thinking and culture will generally have little effect on the learning and teaching within a classroom. If nothing changes, then everything stays the same. Entering an accessible and adaptive classroom is as much about how it feels to be in this kind of learning environment as it is about what you can see and hear happening. Have you ever been into a school where you feel at home and that the learning seems to come alive, jumping off the walls and out of the spaces? We argue that there are some common principles which make an adaptive and accessible learning environment come to life. Here are some key principles of the Central Logo Design that could be applied to your learning environment:

- *There is nothing more important than knowing your learners.* There is no short cut to knowing your learners and developing a strong relationship with them. Whilst we will not necessarily understand or like everyone we meet in our professional life, developing a respectful relationship with our learners is important in many ways. We can begin to explore and promote their interests and understand better their own situation and the bearing this may have on their school life. There is an atmosphere of mutual respect in an accessible and adaptable classroom.

- *Shifting the focus from what learners cannot do to what they can do.* This seems obvious but much educational practice focuses on what learners cannot do and limits their opportunity to access rich discussion and a varied curriculum. Consider learners who are only given access to a certain type of worksheet or activity. Are these learners being given full access to a varied and rich curriculum? Are they actually accessing a different curriculum to other learners? An adaptable and accessible learning environment should not limit anyone's achievement. Teaching Standard 1 (DfE, 2021) states we must set high expectations for our learners that stretch and challenge them whilst maintaining mutual respect. A cultural shift to thinking everyone can achieve will raise the expectation not only within the environment but also for the learner themselves. Conversely, when we focus on what learners cannot do, this can resist expectation.

- *Learners engage in debugging.* As discussed in Chapter 2, Assessment, debugging is an essential aspect of an adaptable classroom. Debugging can be thought of as the process of identifying and ironing out errors from a concept, process or algorithm.

- *A belief that learning and knowledge is not fixed: it develops and grows.* Knowledge is an ever-changing thing and our learners can create new ways of thinking and learning. Think of the creative ways in which a learner might solve a mathematics problem or an innovative way in which they may plan a science investigation. This suggests that knowledge and ways of thinking and learning change and are not fixed.

- *A dialogical approach is not just seen as positive but absolutely essential.* A classroom in which the teacher spends the majority of the time talking and the learner spends the majority of the time listening is not a learning environment but a teaching environment. Learners need to discuss, argue, debate, converse and even informally chat about what they are learning. This allows them to form ideas and test out theories, investigate concepts and put them into practice. An environment rich in discussion is an adaptable classroom as the flow of ideas is open and can adapt to what is needed.

•   *Learning becomes a mutually dependent activity amongst all learners in an environment.* Learning should not and cannot be an isolated activity and the idea of independent learning seems contrary to how we learn. Of course, there are times when learners need to work alone for maximum concentration, but this often occurs after a period of high-quality peer engagement. Thus, learning is always a mutually beneficial and dependent enterprise.

•   *Everyone is learning, not just the learners.* Often, much discussion in education is around learning and knowing things. This can turn teaching into a transactional process in which the expert (teacher) gives knowledge to a novice (learner). This sits on the premise that teachers have nothing to learn, and students have nothing to teach. This couldn't be less true. Equally, when teachers demonstrate their fallibility and weaknesses, this can be one of the most powerful examples of learning. Asking learners to help us understand or learn something can be a powerful experience for both individuals. When learners find solutions and answers that you did not have this can be exhilarating and can model to learners the joy of learning something from others. Teachers should not have all the solutions, nor should you be expected to.

•   *Teachers are interventionists.* As teachers we can often be guilty of allowing our teaching to get in the way of learning. Can you think of a time when you spent so much time 'teaching' that your learners become bored and disengaged? They simply wanted to get on with the learning process. This demonstrates an important fact: children learn! With or without teachers, children are experts at learning about things that interest them. Therefore, teachers become interventionists. They get involved when something is needed such as a prompt, a scaffold, or when something needs modelling; they ask questions to develop thinking or get involved when learners need assistance when debugging something. Allowing learners to find answers themselves is a powerful way to make learning environments rich in learning rather than teaching. As such, a teacher must adapt to the needs of each learner, depending on their stage of development.

▬ REFLECTIVE ACTIVITY ▬

Considering the elements discussed above, engage in an analysis of your own learning environment or an environment you may be studying in. Based on this, consider the following three areas:

(Continued)

(Continued)

- *strengths*: what do you consider to be the strengths of your environment so far?

- *weaknesses*: what are the weaknesses of your environment?

- *opportunities*: based on the above weaknesses what would you address and work on to improve the learning environment? What could you continue to develop and make even stronger about your strengths?

CREATING ADAPTIVE LEARNING EXPERIENCES

Above we have discussed some possible features of an adaptable and accessible learning environment, focusing on relationships and building a culture in the environment. However, we argue it is equally important to reinforce this culture with the activities that take place within that learning environment. So how do we create accessible and adaptive learning experiences in our classrooms and environments? We use the word 'experiences' very deliberately here. We often diminish learning to a set of activities in the classroom. This could be completing a worksheet or set of questions. Much of our educational activity focuses so much on producing something that we lose or forget the value of the process. And yet, the process is where learning takes place; it is very rarely in the product. Here we are trying to change our learners' and our own relationship to knowledge and learning. As long as our learning is overly focused on producing something rather than the experience and process of learning, we will continue to reinforce the idea that school is about getting answers correct. Remember a time you learnt to do something. Perhaps it was learning a skill such as cooking or learning a new sport such as swimming. It is the process that matters. Of course, everyone enjoys the product at the end – for example, the meal – but this is not where the learning has taken place. Researching and finding ingredients, testing cooking techniques, reflecting and critiquing the process is where the learning takes place and debugging happens. Therefore, we need to shift our focus away from the product of our learning and teaching as the most important factor to improving the quality and experience of the learning process.

CREATING EXPANSIVE LEARNING EXPERIENCES

One way in which Papert's (1980) ideas have been taken forward is with the idea of low-threshold, high-ceiling activities. NRich (2019) states:

> *A low threshold, high ceiling (LTHC) task offers the opportunity for everyone to get started and everyone to get stuck. However, in reality, the task alone is not enough. An LTHC classroom is one in which the teacher has an LTHC approach, which implies a certain pedagogy as well as the use of LTHC tasks.*

(n.p.)

This quote is useful because it helps us understand the ways in which these ideas have already been implemented in various subject areas. However, we have decided to expand upon this definition, taking into consideration other aspects of an adaptive learning and teaching philosophy. We have decided to call the activities that take place in these learning environments expansive learning experiences (ELEs). We do this for several reasons. Firstly, we call them *expansive* because these activities should be planned to be as academically expansive as possible. This means, as much as is feasible, experiences should be such that everyone can be working on the same learning idea, accessing it regardless of their academic or personal ability. We shall explore this in more depth below. Secondly, we have moved away from activities or tasks as this has a narrowing effect on what constitutes learning. For example, we know that learning does not *just* happen when learners are just completing a worksheet or engaging in an activity in their formal exercise book. Learning experiences can be extremely varied and we encourage teachers to think about the different ways in which learning can take place. Thus, learning experiences can be anything, but often have the following characteristics to them.

- *Experiences that everyone can access.* A key feature of Papert's work was the idea that learning should be accessible for everyone. Providing learning experiences that everyone can access, progress through and find challenging is the key to an adaptive learning environment and experience. For example, instead of giving learners separate tasks or ideas to be working on, try to create a learning experience in which everyone can work together. A simple example of this would be asking learners how many ways they can make the number 10. Whilst this seems simple, it has incredible scope for expansion. Some learners can be simply thinking about numbers bonds to 10 (9+1, 8+2, etc.), utilising counters and other manipulatives if necessarily. Other learners may think about fractions which may add to 10 (a half plus nine and a half), whilst others may be thinking about complex decimals that could add to 10. In all cases, the learners are working on making the number 10, but each learner can access this task in a way that is appropriate and stimulating to them.

- *Experiences that everyone can find challenging.* As teachers we are expected to stretch and challenge our learners (DfE, 2021), so it is essential that built into any learning experience is the opportunity to find something challenging, where we could potentially get stuck. Whilst we may think that certain learners will not be able to access a task, this is built on an idea that learners and children remain fixed day-to-day. The CCF (2019b) states learners are likely to learn at different rates at different times and accommodation should be made for this understanding.

- *Experiences that produce different outcomes.* Another feature of these experiences would be the possibility for offering various ways to demonstrate learning that has taken place. This can be likened to Tomlinson's (2014) idea of differentiation by product. Whilst some teachers have taken this to mean that every learner should produce an outcome or product that is suited to their academic level, an adaptive approach would allow learners to choose a way of expressing their learning. For example, some learners may choose to express their understanding in a verbal way or through using physical materials and artefacts to articulate a point. Having multiple outcomes to the learning is possible and a variety of expressions of learning should be valued.

- *Can be accessed at different paces and take work to different depths at different times.* As we discuss in Chapter 7, Cognition and metacognition, teachers will have some nuanced understanding of the cognitive needs of the learners in their classroom communities through ongoing formative assessment. As such, they recognise that learners will access and engage with learning at different paces and in different ways based on these needs. Learning experiences should cater for the varying level of cognitive demand that is present and should avoid cognitive overload. Whilst teachers should avoid creating different tasks and differentiating as discussed above they will think about how the depth of the learning may need to be altered or how the scaffolding for success will need to be adjusted.

- *The process of providing a solution or debugging becomes more important than the solution or outcome itself.* Imagine a learning experience in which you expect learners to find bugs or errors in a process or solution to a problem. Not only does this allow learners to demonstrate their understanding of a concept but the level of thinking needed to engage is of a much greater depth. Equally, learners can be extremely creative in the ways in which they debug something, using different methods and avenues to do so. It is also possible that in discussing and considering misconceptions, other misconceptions in a learner's thinking may arise. This was discussed in more detail in Chapter 2, Assessment.

- *Allow learners to experiment with higher-order thinking.* The common belief is that limiting particular learners to certain types of material or content is often an unintended consequence of differentiating in the classroom. It soon becomes clear that different groups of learners are actually accessing completely different curricula. All learners should be exposed to a wide range of content, but also to learning experiences which encourage them to use high-level thinking skills such as critique of and application of ideas. If not, we may find certain learners will never even be exposed to these ideas and skills, let alone have a chance to implement them in their own learning.

- *Are rich in discussion.* The CCF (DfE, 2019b, p. 18) states that 'high-quality classroom talk can support pupils to articulate key ideas, consolidate understanding and extend their vocabulary'. Alexander (2020) has argued that often dialogue and talking in learning is incidental rather than explicit and deliberate. Discussion is therefore essential in learning experiences as it helps learners develop their argumentation and thinking in the process of learning. An expansive learning experience should therefore utilise dialogue to maximise the possibility of securing understanding as well as debugging errors in the process. This also means that learners should experience a range of different sources of dialogue, coming from different teachers and learning peers in the classroom. Flexibly grouping pupils, as advocated for in the CCF, can ensure learners are exposed to a wide range of dialogue in a learning environment.

- *Are not easily finished.* As argued, much of the learning that takes place in our classroom is focused on producing something, on a product, and less on the process. Therefore, we have become hooked on 'finishing' something. Finishing a worksheet, finishing a task, finishing a lesson. A complete shift of culture is needed here where the aim objective of learning is not to finish something but to consider the learning that has taken place. Of course, some of our learners will struggle with this. We can all think of a learner whose sole aim is to get through an activity. ELEs focus on activities that are not easily finished and where learning does not have an 'end'.

- *Are varied in their level of abstraction.* Noted psychologist and educationalist Bruner (1964) suggested that learners must have access to three forms of representation for them to develop a solid understanding of a concept: enactive representation (physical), iconic representation (pictorial) and symbolic representation (abstract). For an ELE to be effective it should offer a range of representations for learners to experience, with the enactive representation coming first. If we think of how we learnt to ride a bike as a child, we did this through trying to ride a bike, not reading a manual on how do to so. Similarly, learners must have an opportunity to explore an idea before translating it into increasingly abstract forms of knowledge and understanding.

- *Place the responsibility on the learner.* Teachers' Standard 2 (DfE, 2021) states we must encourage pupils to take responsibility for their own work and study; however, this is difficult to achieve when learning experiences have little relevance or interest for our learners. Can you imagine taking a genuine interest in something that has little relevance to your life and you find anything but interesting? Therefore, giving learners responsibility through ELEs is crucial.

- *Meaningful and real experiences.* We often spend a great deal of time producing fabricated and irrelevant tasks for our learners to complete which have little bearing on their lives or experiences. It is no wonder their motivation to complete and engage with such tasks is left wanting. Instead, tying experiences to the interests and experiences of our learners as much as possible will make some measure of impact on how meaningful the activity is for our learners.

- *Have progression built into them.* Another feature of these learning experiences is that they are designed in such a way that they naturally have progression built into them. These will be exemplified in the case study below. Making a slight change to the task can help to make it open for progression due to the nature of the task and the variety of possibilities that are present for solution.

- *May involve an activity selection.* Creating an activity menu (many opportunities for learners to demonstrate their understanding – just as a seed will germinate in many different ways, so too does a learner express their understanding in many different ways). This will also increase the level of responsibility and autonomy of the learner.

- *Are rooted in and informed by ongoing assessment for learning.* Finally, all ELEs are rooted in a deep understanding of where a learner is on their learning journey. Without a solid understanding of this and where the learner is going, it is likely we will be unable to intervene in the right way or, even worse, perpetuate misconceptions in the learner's understanding. The CCF (2019b, p. 23) states that 'effective assessment is critical to teaching because it provides teachers with information about pupils' understanding and needs'. We believe the key word here is 'effective' (see Chapter 2, Assessment).

Look at the case study below describing a lesson from KS2. Consider the features of an ELE discussed above and consider how this lesson is an example of ELEs and also how it might be improved through some of the features discussed.

CASE STUDY

Filtering water lesson

Year 5 national curriculum objective: use knowledge of solids, liquids and gases to decide how mixtures might be separated, including through filtering, sieving and evaporating.

Ms James is trying to incorporate ELEs into their classroom to make their teaching and learning as adaptive as possible. They want to ensure there are high expectations of their learners and everyone feels they are part of the same lesson. The class are currently working on a project thinking about clean water and have recently been thinking about water pollution in the United Kingdom. Ms James asks the learners to think about and plan how they would take some dirty water and make it clean. They begin the lesson by asking them to think of a plan of how they might do this. There is a range of materials on the table for them to handle and explore which may be useful. The lesson begins with dialogue and learners move around the classroom. Ms James continues to move around the classroom listening to the conversations happening. They make notes and interject when they notice something interesting and important. They also make notes on a whiteboard for further reference later. The learners are in mixed-ability groups but move freely around at this point in the lesson.

FINAL THOUGHTS

Creating adaptable learning environments may seem complicated and complex but we believe it will be worth your effort to consider this in some detail. Moving away from differentiating learners, which has been shown to have disadvantages, to a more inclusive and open environment will raise expectations and engagement. Utilising Seymour Papert's Central Logo Design model as a way to start thinking about this shift will be an exciting and interesting journey. Whilst we acknowledge other ways of thinking about learning environment are important, we have offered one particular way of reconceptualising this, focusing on prioritising relationships, fostering a culture of collaboration, and emphasising learning as a dynamic and shared activity. We also have to ensure we reinforce this adaptive learning environment with appropriate activities. We advocate challenging the conventional approach of focusing on the end product of learning and advocate for a shift towards valuing the learning process. ELEs, which are academically expansive, accessible to all learners and offer various ways to demonstrate learning, are characterised by the ability to challenge everyone, produce different outcomes, allow for different paces and depths of engagement, and prioritise the process of finding solutions and overcoming misconceptions. By doing this we shall ensure that our learning environments become rich in conjecture, discussion and enquiry and continue to be rooted in high-quality assessment for learning.

KEY TAKEAWAYS

- Creating an adaptive learning environment is more than a simple tokenistic gesture; it is a change of culture and thinking in a school and classroom. It takes time and careful reflection on the pedagogy and culture which already exists within the classroom to make the changes needed.

- As a beginning teacher it is likely you might adopt some of the strategies discussed above and wait for your practice to develop before fully expanding on these ideas.

- Moving away from teaching activities, such as over-reliance on worksheets, to learning experiences is a big shift and can be a scary one, especially for new teachers. Focusing on learning rather than teaching means redesigning how we encourage our learners to express their understanding and communicate this to us as teachers and their peers.

FURTHER READING AND RESOURCE

Boaler, J., Wiliam, D. and Brown, M. (2000) Students' experiences of ability grouping: Disaffection, polarisation and the construction of failure. *British Educational Research Journal*, 26(5), 631–48.

5

SCAFFOLDING

┌─ **CHAPTER OBJECTIVES** ───

After engaging with this chapter, you will be able to:

- understand the importance of the use of scaffolding in your teaching;
- understand the different scaffolding approaches that you could use;
- have confidence in implementing a range of scaffolding withing your teaching practice.

INTRODUCTION

One of the key support mechanisms in any classroom is the use of scaffolding. This can include a wide range of approaches from visual aids such as planning sheets and verbal support linked to questioning through to written step-by-step toolkits, breaking down an activity or a task into its constituent parts.

Scaffolding, above all, should be an interactive process which involves active engagement and participation from both the teacher and the pupil and is most widely recognised as enabling a learner to complete a task that they might not be able to tackle independently without support. This chapter will consider a range of different methods that can be adopted to support practice and will encourage reflection on the potential impact, specifically within the sphere of adaptive teaching.

THE ROLE OF THE TEACHER

Above all else, adaptive teaching is, ultimately, responsive teaching and knowing the individual learner, with a depth of understanding and compassion. When considering how a child builds confidence to tackle a task independently, Vygotsky's ZPD (1978) is recognised as a good starting point as a concept in educational psychology whereby we can reflect upon how the guidance of a more knowledgeable other – the teacher, teaching assistant or a more confident peer – can help to support an individual to complete a task. Another way to consider the ZPD is aligned to the notion of learning potential and the belief that this is most successful when there is an effective level of collaboration between the more knowledgeable other and the learner. Such specific classroom pedagogy, including modelled teaching and the provision of resources, will be explored later in this chapter.

The ZPD is defined by Vygotsky (1978) as 'the distance between the actual developmental level as determined by independent problem solving and the level of potential develop-ment as determined through problem solving under adult guidance or in collaboration with more capable peers' (p. 86). At its very heart, the focus on ZPD is a social idea and it is useful to reflect upon how this is achieved in a whole-class scenario. According to Smit et al. (2013), the concept of responsiveness supports the adaptive nature of scaffolding; moreover, it is argued to be at the very heart of the scaffolding process.

For Wood et al. (1976) there are six key actions carried out by the teacher to enable success:

1. *Recruiting interest in the task*

2. *Simplifying the task*

3. *Maintaining direction towards the goals of the task*

4. *Marking critical features*

5. *Controlling frustration*

6. *Modelling the preferred procedures by demonstrating, so that the learner can imitate it back.*

(p. 98)

REFLECTIVE ACTIVITY

Consider the six key actions above. Reflect upon a lesson that you have recently delivered or observed being facilitated by a colleague.

Can you identify the ways in which you incorporated each area into your teaching or are there aspects of this practice that could form the beginnings of an action plan for future teaching?

As confidence builds when tackling an activity, the amount of support given should be reduced so that, eventually, children can work towards independence and achieve a sense of success. Scaffolding should be seen as a process in which a pupil is building an ability to develop their understanding, not just focusing upon the final output of completing a piece of work – here the emphasis is on learning, not simply teaching. With this in mind, the specifics of the scaffolding should be adapted for different groups and individuals, rather than providing different content for different learners, as is often seen with the differen-tiation of tasks and fixed grouping (see Chapter 3). According to Wass and Golding (2014), giving students the most challenging tasks that they can access with the support of carefully curated scaffolding leads to the greatest learning gains. It is also interesting to consider how using well-constructed and adaptive scaffolding with children who have specific challenges with their own learning encourages a greater sense of autonomy as independent learners and leads to an increased motivation and responsibility for attempting more demanding tasks.

This chapter will offer three different concepts of scaffolding to be used within an adaptive environment: *visual* (incorporating modelled examples of work and the use of specific resources), *verbal* (supported speaking and listening activities with a focus on collaboration and highlighting previous learning) and *written* scaffolds (writing frames), along with specific examples for you to develop and adapt for your setting.

THE CULTURE OF SCAFFOLDING: SELF-EFFICACY AND THE LEARNING ENVIRONMENT

The DfE established the minimum requirements for teachers' practice in their *Teachers' Standards* document (2021). Part One includes reference to teachers being required to: 'Set high expectations which inspire, motivate and challenge pupils' (p. 10), suggesting that this is achieved by establishing a mutually respectful, safe and stimulating environment; setting goals which stretch and challenge all; and that a teacher should demonstrate the attitudes, values and behaviour which are expected of pupils (DfE, 2021). Those learning environments that consider each learner as an individual and where children are offered a safe and supportive place to learn will help children to feel empowered to take risks and have a go. All too often, children who are identified as SEN are given help and adaptations to catch up, rather than being provided with opportunities to challenge them in their own learning; this is commonly seen in the format of intervention activities and differentiated work. In this context, the gap of knowledge gets wider and opportunities to explore newly acquired learning are severely limited.

In order to overcome this, when creating an activity, teachers should be secure as to what the intention of the lesson is, and what support can be employed to ensure success for all. Within this approach, all children should be given the opportunity to demonstrate how they have secured the next phase of their learning and how this can be explored further in a more independent way in future lessons, enabling a sense of achievement and promoting a growth mindset.

Classroom culture is key, Hattie (2012) explores the concept of how high respect for pupils from their teachers links to high levels of pupil success, and although this may seem obvious, it is an essential ingredient of adaptive classroom culture. According to Hattie (2012), before planning any learning activity, it is vital to appreciate what a pupil knows already and how this knowledge can be used to extend understanding and progress.

What a student brings to the classroom each year is very much related to his or her achieve-
ment in previous years: brighter students tend to achieve more, and not-so-bright students
achieve less. Our job as teacher is to mess this up, by planning ways in which to accelerate
the growth of those who start behind, so that they can most efficiently attain the curriculum
and learning objectives of the lessons alongside the brightest students.

(2012, p. 38)

Self-efficacy plays an important role in the process of learning, for children to be able to make connections within their own learning scaffolding is a vital part of the process. The strength of belief that a learner has in their own potential is fragile and delicate, easily broken and difficult to repair.

— REFLECTIVE ACTIVITY —

Think about a child that you have taught in the past who you recognise as having low self-esteem.

Why might such a learner be avoidant of more challenging tasks, and how can this be managed?

It is essential that all teachers are aware of what every child in the class is thinking and, importantly, what they know already as a starting point for their learning. A supportive classroom will harness the power of self-efficacy as a motivational tool and encourage a growth mindset approach that actively encourages an ethos of setting out clearly steps for success. Those identified as having a positive strength of belief or high personal self-esteem tend to embrace misconceptions and mistakes and use these as a way to learn for future tasks. As Hattie and Larsen (2020) suggest,

If we want to 'know' our students then we do need to better understand how they are thinking,
how they are processing the nature of the task, how they are tackling the problem, what their
misconceptions are, how they move to success, and much more. This is what we need to be
more visible to then know how to teach more effectively.

(p. 37)

DISMANTLING THE SCAFFOLDING

Careful consideration must be given to the implementation of scaffolding; teachers must be aware of the implications of how a learner can become overly reliant upon support and that the reassuring and guiding concept of scaffolding itself could endanger creativity and independence, with a detrimental impact upon the overall learning of the child. Therefore, scaffolding should be given a health warning – clear messaging here is imperative. Classrooms should be a place of support, but also a place where learners are enabled to employ their own personal strategies to meet their needs. This can be successfully achieved by being clear and specific about the learning taking place and the steps to success for achieving the outcome of the lesson, empowering learners by boosting their self-efficacy and resilience with specific direct modelling alongside high-quality teaching facilitated by a teacher who understands their learners, so that they are able to gradually reduce the support with a view to achieving independence – although it is important to recognise that this may not be achievable for all in every learning environment.

Fading or the gradual withdrawal of scaffolding is naturally dependent upon the individual child, their specific needs, experiences and self-efficacy. According to van de Pol et al. (2010), scaffolding evolves around three main phases:

- *contingent*: where a teacher adapts support to suit the needs of a learner; this is identified after student ability is assessed via observation or questioning and the careful monitoring of levels of understanding;

- *fading or the gradual withdrawal of scaffolding*: dependent upon a pupil's grasp of a specific concept;

- *transfer of responsibility*: where the ownership of a particular skill or outcome becomes the responsibility of the learner.

Crucially, this model places scaffolding within the context of a teaching method, rather than an approach to simply complete a stand-alone task. This could be a shift in approach within some classroom environments, but would bring with it reward in terms of learning and the 'stickability' of knowledge as children are able to appreciate their own needs as a learner.

REFLECTIVE ACTIVITY

Think about the three phases of scaffolding according to van de Pol et al. (2010) and the pedagogical approaches you have observed or taught in practice.

- How confident are you when considering the contingent phase? How do you (or observed colleagues) implement formative assessment and adapt scaffolding according to need?

- Can you think of an example when you or a colleague consciously 'faded' scaffolding as a learning sequence evolved? Did this look the same for all learners or was this adapted to suit individual need? Was the fading child led?

- How do you ensure that all children experience a transfer of responsibility as a learner and, indeed, is this actually possible for all learners all of the time?

VISUAL SCAFFOLDING

WORKING WALLS

Working walls provide an opportunity for ongoing support throughout a sequence of work. These tend to be focused upon the core areas of English and maths; however, foundation subjects should not be overlooked, and these subjects can be interwoven successfully within a cross-curricular approach. The use of classroom displays has evolved over the years as a greater emphasis upon modelling specific taught strategies has become a priority within the curriculum. Reflecting the current teaching and learning sequence, effective learning walls should be embedded within the classroom culture; the resources should be added in lessons and link to the teaching of that specific activity – for example, sharing key story vocabulary in English or helping the children to identify the symbols of greater, less than or equal to in maths. It is interesting to see the vast array of 'ready-made' working walls available on the internet, beautifully themed in colours and design, but a word of caution here: working walls are intended to be an evolving and working resource – Post-it notes, whiteboards, photocopies of good examples of sentence starters and hand-drawn calculations would demonstrate an adaptive evolution of ideas and modelling, rather than a pristine, laminated display which is passive and one-sided in its approach and limited in its scope to get children directly involved in their learning.

Features of an effective working wall can include:

- *the objective for the sequence of learning*: this is an opportunity to demonstrate what learners will be able to achieve at the end of the unit;

- *community vocabulary*: this can be added to as the sequence progresses and is effective when child led, with the main words and phrases being provided by the teacher at the start of the learning. As the children begin to work independently, their ideas can be included so that others can 'magpie' the words, developing a growing and flourishing vocabulary. Unknown technical vocabulary, in particular, can cause anxiety in learners; by offering an *aide memoire* in this way, the children have an ongoing reminder throughout their sequence of work;

- *examples of children's work*: not just final pieces but work in progress;

- *examples of misconceptions or errors in work*: choosing examples that illustrate how a learner has responded to a marking comment by revisiting their work and editing or correcting reinforces the link between assessment and making steps to progress. It will support an ethos in the classroom where mistakes and revisiting to make improvements are part of the learning process, in turn supporting the notion of self-esteem and self-efficacy.

Working walls should be updated each day to demonstrate how the learning within a topic is evolving – including photographs of the children on their learning journey. They should be personalised to the learning that is taking place within a specific learning environment and consider the needs of learners in the particular classroom setting.

Working walls must be seen as evolutionary – keep a specific framework in mind when creating the visual scaffold, identify what the children already know, what it is that they will be learning in this sequence to develop their understanding further; identify the different steps that will be taken along the learning process – the learning outcome will then provide an endpoint of their learning.

Interactive opportunities can be created as part of a working wall. Consider how practical resources can form part of the structure of support; this could be activities that the children use independently – for example, prompt cards, games and resources that can effectively scaffold the learning.

CASE STUDY

After a recent Ofsted inspection, Green Bank Primary School is reflecting upon ways in which to provide a more clear and consistent approach to scaffolding children's learning - specifically in the core areas of maths and English - and also upon how cross-curricular subjects can be interwoven into this focus. In the past, individual teachers created working walls in their classrooms as a way in which to consolidate learning and share key guidance for the children to follow as a sequence of learning develops. However, this had not been enacted by all staff and some of the resources were not updated regularly where a working wall was provided. The inspection noted the effective practice of visual support in the Key Stage 1 classrooms and praised some practitioners for their provision - notably how they provided key vocabulary, modelled examples and stem sentences. But there was a lack of consistency across the school, particularly in upper Key Stage 2, and this was highlighted as something to reflect upon further. Inspectors noted how the children in Year 1 and Year 2 found the working walls in their classroom helpful and that they supported them in putting together their recent work on story writing and gave them ideas on how to make their work even better. It was suggested that a consistent approach in each classroom would develop a climate for more focused scaffolding and ongoing support and, as a result, outputs would improve as children's confidence as writers increased. Subject leaders were tasked with moving this priority forwards, taking note of good practice and developing strategies throughout the school.

The key reflections for the school following the discussion with the inspector were:

* how do children know what their steps of learning will be?

* how can the teachers demonstrate what the children already know and how do they ensure that all children feel confident as new steps to learning are introduced?

* how do the children know that they are going to reach a more independent point in their learning whilst having a clear idea of what the over-arching aim of the sequence is?

━━ **REFLECTIVE ACTIVITY** ━━━

How could you use working walls as a way to scaffolding learning in a sequence of work?

How could working walls provide evidence for the questions identified above?

How do you think that working walls can contribute to the overall ethos of an adaptive class-room environment and how can they be created to specifically promote high expectations for all learners?

How can misconceptions be addressed and challenged with a working wall and, impor-tantly, how can you demonstrate ways to overcome such misconceptions in a supportive and scaffolded way?

USING MANIPULATIVES

Manipulatives are a physical object that can be used to explore an abstract concept; this is often employed in mathematics – resources include counters and blocks. The case study below illustrates the use of such objects to support learning.

━━ **CASE STUDY** ━━━

Context, Year 2 maths: solving addition and subtraction word problems. This is the final lesson in a sequence of learning, where the children have investigated the formal methods of calculation. In the middle of the tables are question cards, each with a word problem that could include a one- or two-step problem for them to solve. The children are seated in mixed-ability groups and are able to choose their own questions, which vary in the level of challenge, from the centre of the table; they are encouraged to work with a partner should they wish. Each table has a toolkit of manipulative resources that are available for the children to access in every lesson; this comprises of Numicon®, coun-ters, base ten blocks, dice, place-value frames and hundred squares. These resources have been interwoven into the strategies modelled to the children throughout the unit of work, so the children feel confident in selecting and using the equipment if they would like to. As the learning has progressed during the sequence the teacher 'fades' the use of the resources when modelling in order to minimise the risk of over-reliance; however, the tool-kits are still available on the table for the children to access. In this lesson, some children have the confidence to tackle the questions independently and without the support of a resource, whereas some of the class do access the toolkit – there is no stigma attached to this as the equipment is always present, it is part of the classroom, just like a pencil pot.

It is interesting to note that the maths toolbox is a whole-school approach, from Reception right through to Year 6, so it contributes to the culture of learning, encouraging children to take control of their own scaffolding approaches and enabling them to become

(Continued)

(Continued)

invested in managing their own learning: the resources are there if they are needed, but there is no compulsion to use them. Teachers are mindful of the reluctance of older children, in particular, to access supportive resources; however, the culture of the school has been carefully created to ensure that this is not an issue. In the nursery provision at this school, for example, the children are encouraged to engage with free play of manipulative resources, including Numicon® and threaded beads, so that they simply become familiar with the feel of the objects before their understanding of number is explored more formally. In Year 6, children are encouraged to use visual representations in their calculations to demonstrate the process they have followed to reach an answer.

After the lesson, some children in Year 2 were asked about how they used the toolkits.

Child A: 'The toolkit helps me to feel stronger with my learning because I can see how the numbers work; this can be difficult to do in my head. I remember how we used the cubes to work out subtraction the other day and I feel happy that I can use the same things to help me on my own. My teacher has examples on the whiteboard and uses the same things like cubes; it is funny when he drags them over the screen to show us, it's the same as what we do!'

Child B: 'I don't really need the toolkit, but sometimes it helps me when the questions get tough, especially the tricky questions that I do. I like to challenge myself with hard work but I know that I can go back and use a hundred square to remind me of the numbers if I need to.'

REFLECTIVE ACTIVITY

- What are the challenges in the case study? Remember that scaffolds are regarded as a temporary support and that they should be 'faded' and eventually removed as a level of independence is reached.

- How could this approach lead to a dependence upon scaffolding resources and how can this be avoided?

- How would you define the culture in your current setting linked to use of specific scaffolding approaches?

- When using scaffolding tools such as manipulatives, writing frameworks or specific representations for an activity, how do you ensure that the children reflect upon their use as a learning sequence evolves, specifically moving towards independence?

WRITTEN SCAFFOLDING

WRITING FRAMES

Written scaffolds are beneficial when the specific focus is a writing task; they often form part of a modelling input and can be included as part of a working wall. Writing frames are frequently used to provide a structure for learners to follow; they can include a skeleton format and key words and phrases for a specific genre.

As highlighted earlier, Vygotsky (1978) believed that children begin to learn a new concept thanks to the input of an expert other; this relationship then shifts to a greater level of independence as the child has opportunities to explore, practise, refine and achieve and is enabled by the expert, who continues to guide. However, in a classroom of 30 individual learners, providing support in an individualised way is often a significant challenge. Scaffolding writing with a model such as a writing frame is a way of providing support without the expert other being directly involved at every step of the writing process and limiting individual creativity (Wray and Lewis, 1997).

In order for writing frames to be used successfully, first, the teacher must ensure that the children are confident with the particular text type – by sharing examples of model texts, spending time highlighting the key features and exploring the authorial intent of the piece. A good example for this would be newspaper articles for a recount text; here the format is specific – the layout of a newspaper article is very definite and should include a heading, subheading, an introductory paragraph, the main body should be in chronological order and a quote is always useful in adding to the overall feel of the piece. Children should have the opportunity to engage with real-life examples so that they appreciate the authenticity and purpose of the text type. In terms of an adaptive response, all of the children should have the opportunity to be immersed in the specific text language and the teacher should have high expectations; as always, the final outcome should be shared so that all learners are clear as to what they are working towards.

When the children are comfortable with the genre and time has been given to discussion around the text type, the teacher can then model writing as a scaffold and the learners can then begin to co-construct their own piece, either with an adult or a peer; the emphasis here is on oral rehearsal and an articulation of choices, including specific vocabulary and sentence structure – again, a working wall can help here to pull ideas together. Wray and Lewis (1997) suggest that teachers could use frames when they model and co-construct with the learners, demonstrating the process and adding another layer of support into the process. When asking a learner to write independently, they can use a provided scaffolding frame as a skeleton so that their focus can be primarily on the vocabulary and other key features, rather than solely focusing on the format of the genre.

In line with the essence of scaffolding, it is essential to consider how writing frames can provide adaptive and timely support for all learners; careful thought must be given to the 'fading' of this approach. Interestingly, Wray and Lewis (1997) note that although frames are an excellent way to scaffold whole-class modelling, the scaffold should be used for those learners who feel the need for a structured support – they are not required for those children who are already able to write with confidence within a known text type. As with all adaptive approaches, the opportunity for children to be use a specific resource should they wish to is the focus, rather than it being a support for a complete sequence of learning. If careful teaching is deconstructed into steps for success in which all learners can understand and feel supported along the way, the outcome will be a positive one.

Bearne and Reedy (2018) highlight the importance of a child's intrinsic motivation to write being a key to successful authorship of any text type; scaffolds should allow the writer's voice to be heard and not restrict creativity or independent thought. If a teacher spends time modelling, sharing and talking, the child will feel enabled, supported and, finally, able to independently explore and write. When trawling through children's workbooks, all too often outputs of writing are prescribed and fixed and this, it could be argued, is the result of over-reliance on supportive strategies. As with everything, a balance is key – as Bearne and Reedy suggest, 'whilst story maps, frames and scaffolds can be helpful, it is important to allow children's written creativity space to breathe' (2018, p. 322). It is clear that scaffolding can, however, reduce vulnerability and empower a feeling of resilience; in creating and nurturing this kind of learning environment, learners are more likely to take a risk.

CASE STUDY

Using writing frames and the progression through a teaching sequence: A Year 3 class was focusing on instructional texts with the aim that, at the end of the sequence, the children would write an independent piece linked to their class story, *The Boy Who Grew Dragons*, by Andy Shepherd. A working wall was created with key vocabulary for instructional texts, such as a bank of imperative verbs and examples of real-life instructions, including images. Time was given to reflect upon prior learning and to draw upon previous experiences linked to instructional texts. During the first lesson in the sequence, the learners were given examples of instructional texts to explore; the priority was to ensure that they felt comfortable in identifying the many possible features. The teacher provided different formats, including building flat-pack furniture that used minimal language so as not to restrict the learners' understanding and to ensure that the children recognise that instructional texts are more than recipes or a step-by-step guide. Following on from this, the children completed practical sequencing activities, following instructional texts that were effective and some that had key information missing or were ambiguous in their approach. The children had a strong understanding of effective instructional texts thanks to the previous sessions, so were able to make judgements on success or limitations and, importantly, offer ways to improve the texts. Teacher modelling was a thread throughout this stage and the working wall was used to add good examples throughout.

Using the writing frame below, the children used the scaffold to write their own instructional text relating to the opportunity they had to plant spring bulbs in the school sensory garden. They were able to use the experience that they had to impart their knowledge to the Year 4 class, who were going to complete the same task in their forest school session - thus, there was a clear purpose for their writing. Key words were given; however, it is important to note that there was space allocated for the children to add their own words should they wish. At this point in the learning sequence, the children had been fully immersed in the language and tone of the text so were able to add their own authentic voice to the piece; for those who were less confident, linking the practical lived experience to the narrative was well supported by the vocabulary and, of course, the working wall.

Table 5.1   Example of a writing frame

Instructional text		
How to plant daffodil bulbs		
Some useful key words:	Some useful instructional text vocabulary:	
daffodil	first	place
bulb	then	take
compost	next	
trowel	finally	
gloves	push	
watering can	carefully	
What you will need: * * * *	Introduction:	
Instructions: Step 1: Step 2: Step 3: Step 4:		

The culmination of this sequence was the final piece of independent writing with the children - a set of imaginary instructions explaining how they looked after their special dragon plant, linked to the class text. The task required both imagination and a secure understanding of the book, using the framework of instructional vocabulary logical order, but enhanced with creativity and a toolkit of fictional devices that were a thread that ran through the teaching of English in the classroom. For this piece, the first lesson was a planning session and the children were encouraged to create their own framework to use. There was a variety of scaffolding grids available for those children who wanted them and the previous examples were still presented on the working wall along with key vocabulary. In pairs, children worked together to orally rehearse and share their ideas before the writing process began.

▬ REFLECTIVE ACTIVITY ▬▬▬▬▬▬▬▬▬▬▬▬▬▬▬▬▬▬▬▬▬▬▬▬▬▬▬▬▬

How can a writing frame be designed to allow for creativity?

Think here about how autonomy for learning can be fostered – paired work can be a helpful tool here.

Consider how you could design a written scaffolding resource similar to the example given that enables the learner to feel secure in the writing task but still empowered to demonstrate their imagination and innovation.

Consider here the use of vocabulary and the steps to success that could be taken before an independent task begins.

How can such a scaffolding tool be 'faded' so as to reduce dependency over time but still leave a legacy of support?

VERBAL SCAFFOLDING

The previous approaches in this chapter, specifically focusing on visual and written scaffolds, share common themes: collaboration and active learning. Creating a safe environment where the teacher is adaptive and responsive contributes to an overall positive learning experience, where children are empowered to try and, importantly, take a risk. Hattie (2012) explores how a notion of respect for pupils from their teachers links to pupil success through basic classroom interactions and a sense of care and commitment. However, this can be extended beyond the relationship of teacher and pupil towards the interconnectedness of pupil-to-pupil dialogue and interaction.

Collaborative skills need to be modelled and taught; this includes active listening and empathy for the views of others. Children need help and opportunities to develop the skills together for such an approach to be effective. A whole-school approach to embedding the skills of collaboration is helpful through all aspects of school life beyond the classroom and should involve all children, regardless of their attainment. The EEF (2018b) emphasises that in order to minimise any gaps, 'support should be provided through well-structured and carefully designed learning activities … if collaborative learning approaches just involve high attaining pupils solving problems with no input from their peers – this is likely to widen existing gaps in attainment'.

THINK, PAIR, SHARE

Think, pair, share is a basic discussion technique which can be used easily to scaffold understanding and allow a learner to respond to an open-ended question before sharing their thoughts with other children. Not only does this approach encourage participation in a session, but it also helps to build confidence and opens learners to wider ideas and different perspectives. Consideration must be given to the relationships in the classroom and, particularly, the dynamics of different learners; clear rules should be established to ensure politeness. Modelling would support with the correct language of how to respond and the teacher must think carefully about how skills are developed in logical and realistic steps. Random pairings are seen as fair and enhance a sense of collaboration; changing the pairings regularly so that the children can work with different peers is also important. However, teachers could have an oversight into how strategic partnerships may be more beneficial.

An example is below:

> *Teacher:* Look at this shape. I would like you to think of a specific property that this example has – keep that idea in your mind.

The children have a minute of thinking time to look at the shape and to individually think about what they can see. They are seated in mixed-ability groups.

> *Teacher:* Now, turn to your partner and share the particular property that you were thinking about.
>
> *Child A:* I can see that this shape has three sides, so I know it is a triangle, and I think all the sides are the same length.
>
> *Child B:* Yes, it is definitely a triangle and I noticed that all the sides are the same length too.
>
> *Child A:* I can't remember the name of the triangles that have the same sides.
>
> *Child B:* It's an equilateral triangle, I remember it because equal means the same.
>
> *Teacher:* Now, I would like you to share one property that you discussed with your partner with the rest of your table.
>
> *Child A:* We noticed that the triangle is an equilateral – we know this because all of the sides are the same length.
>
> *Teacher:* OK, so you have all had a chance to talk on your tables, who would like to share their ideas with the class now?

REFLECTIVE ACTIVITY

Think about a specific lesson that you taught recently.

How many opportunities did you give learners to reflect upon, process and share their thoughts and learning with a peer?

Does your classroom layout facilitate paired talk and, importantly, are there opportunities for further collaboration with other learners from the paired talk start-point?

STEM SENTENCES

In order to enrich and support discussion further, stem sentences can be provided to scaffold responses so that the learner can offer a response without the extra requirement of thinking about how to structure a response. The stem sentences can be orally modelled by the teacher to demonstrate how they can be used effectively. In the EYFS and lower key stages, sentence stems should encourage children to develop their voice; the focus here is supporting and developing emerging speaking and listening skills, including taking turns and speaking audibly:

> *Mr Martin*:   I think that the caterpillar was greedy in the story because at the end he had a tummy ache. What do you think Alfie? Ask Lily, your partner, if she thinks the caterpillar was greedy and why she thinks this.
>
> *Alfie*:   Do you think the caterpillar was greedy?
>
> *Lily*:   Yes, I think so because he ate a lollipop and a pickle!
>
> *Alfie*:   You are right – I think he was greedy too because at the end he had a tummy ache; he ate too much!

As the children progress into Key Stage 1, children should be encouraged to develop their early language strategies to include ways in which to take turns and listen attentively and to ask questions in order to develop the necessary skills of discussion. To achieve this competency, learners must have the opportunity to practise such an exchange after having the skills modelled and introduced explicitly. It is important to allow children to put across their points of view, stating that they either agree or disagree and also building upon the points of view of their peers – for example, 'I hadn't thought about that before you said it, now I think …'

In Key Stage 2, emphasis must be given to an understanding of audience and opportunities to develop and clarify ideas offered by others. This approach can be scaffolded with oral modelling or written examples of sentence starters to structure responses as the skills are embedded over time. Examples could include:

- I agree with you … because …

- I really like your idea because … however …

- I'm not sure that I agree with what you have said because …

- At first, I was thinking about … but now, after listening to you, I think that …

- I have a different idea …

Paired talk can promote skills linked to summarising and clarification – for example, we think that, we agree that, we disagree that and we need to find out more about. For children who are not confident with their own understanding, having the opportunity to share ideas with another learner can boost confidence and reduce anxiety in a whole-class environment; the sentence stems are a key part of this overall scaffolded approach.

FINAL THOUGHTS

This chapter has considered three main types of scaffolding – visual, written and verbal – and contextualised the contribution that each approach can make within an adaptive classroom. When reflecting upon the *Teachers' Standards* (DfE, 2021), it is clear that a teacher should be committed to having high expectations for all learners; scaffolding can play an important role in this in so many ways, from providing resources to conceptualising abstract ideas through to enriching quality dialogue and collaborative discussion, which, in turn, will positively impact both written and verbal outcomes. With care and considera-tion, teachers need to implement scaffolds so that creativity can flourish and over-reliance can be managed. Walking the scaffolding tightrope can be daunting, particularly for begin-ning teachers; however, keeping focused upon the need to create an environment in which learners feel empowered to take a risk and resilient enough to make decisions for them-selves as learners should be reward in itself.

REFLECTIVE ACTIVITY

Have a professional discussion with a colleague about their approaches to the three forms of scaffolding in this chapter.

Ask them to articulate how they overcome the challenges that have been highlighted here and then write a list of considerations that you feel are relevant to your own practice.

Discuss the possibility of peer-to-peer observation, specifically focusing on scaffolding approaches, and revisit the themes identified.

KEY TAKEAWAYS

- Scaffolding can incorporate a number of approaches within an adaptive environment.
- Scaffolding must be managed carefully to mitigate over-reliance and the impact upon autonomous, creative learning.
- A whole-school ethos is helpful for consistency - although this must be adapted for each classroom setting and the needs of its learners.

FURTHER READING AND RESOURCES

Gershon, M. (2017) *50 Quick Ways to Use Scaffolding and Modelling.* Quick 50 Teaching Series, Book 24.

Hattie, J. and Larsen, S.N. (2020) *The Purposes of Education: A Conversation between John Hattie and Steen Nepper Larsen.* Abingdon: Routledge.

Palmer, S. (2010) *Speaking Frames: How to Teach Talk for Writing: Ages 10–14.* London: David Fulton.

6

ADAPTIVE INTERVENTION

CHAPTER OBJECTIVES

After engaging with this chapter, you will be able to:

- contextualise targeted interventions within adaptive teaching and the challenges faced when implementing an intervention;

- reflect upon interventions that you have observed or managed and reflect upon their true effectiveness in terms of adaptation and inclusion;

- consider the importance of monitoring and wider partnerships as part of the intervention process.

INTRODUCTION

Interventions have become integral to the classroom over the years and have evolved to provide support across all aspects of provision, including a specific skill linked to the curriculum, such as reading comprehension, through to a more holistic social-emotional focused intervention. Interventions can be enacted as a quick, reactive response in a lesson, when a teacher – through questioning during the main input of a lesson – recognises that a child is struggling with a concept and acts in the moment to provide more support in an independent activity with a small-group focus in the classroom. Alternatively, it can be a longer-term programme where a learner has a significant gap in knowledge and requires a more structured response beyond the classroom, possibly led by a teaching assistant and scheduled weekly. Interventions, it could be argued, are often seen as a segregationist rather than inclusive in practice, with children being taken away from their classroom and their peers to be instructed separately. This chapter aims to explore academic interventions specifically and will offer the opportunity for reflection on current practice within the context of adaptation.

THE EVOLUTION OF INTERVENTIONS

Interventions have the potential to encompass so many different supportive approaches that contribute to the inclusive nature of a school and are essential in providing adaptive support for children. These often go beyond an academic focus or specific skill and are tailored to a broader need that encompasses the wider needs of a child – for example, issues of self-esteem, social-emotional support, socio-economic challenge or, more recently, the aftermath of the global pandemic. In the past, academic interventions have been targeted at those struggling with aspects of the curriculum and children identified as having special educational needs (SEN); however, the principles of intervention have evolved to include other groups. The Warnock Report (1978) heralded the introduction of SEN and statements of SEN, along with new rights for parents and a greater sense of inclusion within mainstream school, promoting a social model of disability whereby unnecessary barriers are removed rather than the deficit-driven medical model which often leads to low expectations and a focus on the need rather than practical solutions to overcome and support the identified difference. Although the two models are useful, they can make the concept of inclusion too simplified; it is often the case that many schools employ elements of both when designing and implementing intervention approaches. The intent and proposed impact of any support given needs to be clear and well-considered.

▬ CASE STUDY ▬

Simon has been placed into an adult-led, one-to-one reading intervention group at lunch-time because he initiates rough-play, and it was decided that he should have time away from his peers to limit the opportunity for disruptive behaviour. Simon is becoming more frustrated because he feels he is being punished and made to read, rather than having time to play with his friends. In addition, he is becoming frustrated and resentful of the teaching staff and unwilling to co-operate in the intervention session. In class, he is exhibiting withdrawn behaviour and is struggling to concentrate. Friendships are becoming strained, and he is feeling more left out socially.

In this scenario, Simon is receiving a level of adapted support akin to the medical model of inclusion; however, the removal of him from the source of the problem, being outside and being unable to regulate his behaviour, means that it is not being tackled. The intention is that Simon will be reintegrated with other children at some point, but without providing specific targeted support around the root cause of his behaviour the cycle will continue, and Simon will probably be segregated again.

A social solution to the same challenge could be the provision of adult support in the form of a 'play-mentor' who can facilitate and lead activities for all children and be on-hand to step-in should the need arise.

Embedding a philosophy in which all children are welcome as learners and individuals can be a challenge; however, it is imperative that, regardless of the situation, schools should focus on the barriers faced by individuals and what can practically be enacted to ensure that the challenges can be overcome, whether social, emotional, or academic. This is achieved by really knowing your learners and being adaptive in your response to their needs.

Contextually, the many demands within the sphere of education are extensive and have implications beyond the classroom, but making high-quality adaptations and providing opportunities for positive relationships between learners and their teachers and support staff can make a significant difference. According to the EEF (2021), teaching assistants delivering targeted interventions significantly impact attainment – between three and four additional months of progress. However, it is important to note that to achieve such impact, the interventions were structured and supported with quality resources including robust staff training, which will be discussed later (EEF, 2021, p.11).

Guidance and policy have continued to reaffirm the importance of inclusive practice, the *National Curriculum* (DfE, 2013b) states that:

> *Teachers should set high expectations for every pupil. They should plan stretching work for pupils whose attainment is significantly above the expected standard. They have an even greater obligation to plan lessons for pupils who have low levels of prior attainment or come from disadvantaged backgrounds.*
>
> (Paragraph 4.1)

In essence, knowing your students and having a firm understanding of both the curriculum and pedagogical approaches are fundamental when planning interventions; a teacher must also be secure in their own values and personal philosophy as part of this process.

CREATING AN ADAPTIVE LEARNING ENVIRONMENT

Culturally, every school is unique and is a product of the leadership of the setting, the wider local context and environment, the pupils and those who are employed in the many different roles – from site supervisor through to class teachers. From the moment you enter a school reception area, judgements can and will be made about the place as a centre of learning. Very often you are greeted by a welcoming motto and key values of the school, not to mention photographs of the staff or displays showcasing children's creativity. Visiting an inner-city school, I was humbled by a display that included the word 'welcome' written in the languages beyond English spoken by the children who attend the setting and a map that included pins to locate the origin of their families. A community bookcase within the entrance area stored copies of books written in numerous languages that parents could borrow; it was evident from my first few moments in this school that the wider community was welcomed, and the diversity of the population that the school serves was celebrated. Collaboration with colleagues and stakeholders including families and outside agencies within a learning landscape that promotes high expectations for all along with a positive approach towards inclusion and a celebration of diversity makes a significant difference. Glazzard et al. (2010) highlight the importance of providing a learning environment that develops self-esteem, self-worth and confidence along with resilience and a growth mindset and that these are ingredients that support a culture of belonging and a sense that all individuals, regardless of ability or background, are part of one community.

Naturally, professionals' individual values of inclusion are important in shaping and influencing practice, and the *Teachers' Standards* (DfE, 2021) – particularly Part One: Teaching – establish firm guidance, with a recommendation for teachers to be reflective of their personal values and philosophy. They should:

Set high expectations which inspire, motivate and challenge pupils

- *establish a safe and stimulating environment for pupils, rooted in mutual respect*

- *set goals that stretch and challenge pupils of all backgrounds, abilities and dispositions*

- *demonstrate consistently the positive attitudes, values and behaviour which are expected of pupils.*

(DfE, 2021, p. 10)

An inclusive teacher is respectful of difference and provides an environment that allows for responsive adaptations so that everyone has an opportunity to experience success; they are committed to finding new ways of working to support their learners; they have a toolkit of pedagogy and practice to support learning; and work collaboratively with colleagues to establish the optimum learning experience for all. Those teachers who are adept in adapting in the moment and making decisions proactively using quality-first teaching, whilst balancing the guidance and expertise of colleagues, including the school's special educational needs coordinator (SENCO) are rewarded with a classroom in which children make progress and are happy to take a chance with their learning. As the *Special Educational Needs and Disability Code of Practice* (*SEND Code of Practice*) (DfE, 2015) states, 'additional interventions and support cannot compensate for a lack of good quality teaching' (p. 99). Adaptive and responsive interventions that are facilitated within an inclusive environment allow all children to work with their peers and within such a community of practice they can collaborate and enjoy opportunities together (as explored in greater detail in Chapter 3, Grouping).

Along with the *SEND Code of Practice* (DfES, 2015), the Equality Act (2010) defines nine protected characteristics: gender, age, disability, pregnancy and maternity, race, religion or belief, sex, sexual orientation, marriage or civil partnership and, as a result of this, schools are expected to make reasonable adjustments to accommodate these characteristics. It is also important to appreciate that anyone with a connection to a person who is recognised as having a protected characteristic is also safeguarded by the law. According to government data, in 2022/3, over 1.5 million pupils in England have SEN; this is an increase of 87,000 from 2022 (DfE, 2023a). Such statistics demonstrate that there are more children in mainstream schools now than ever before who will require reasonable adjustments and adaptations to ensure they can succeed and make at least expected progress personal to them.

▬ REFLECTIVE ACTIVITY ▬

Consider how the Equality Act (2010) impacts your school setting or schools that you have visited in the past.

Think about what reasonable adjustments look like in the setting within the context of a targeted intervention that you have seen take place. Make a list of the types of approaches that you have seen.

How aware are you of your professional obligation to uphold the legislation and how do you ensure that all those connected to a learner who is protected by the law are also adequately supported?

TYPES OF ACADEMIC INTERVENTION

Garry (2020) helpfully identifies two different approaches that constitute the practice of intervention; this is particularly helpful when defining, planning and implementing a particular approach. Firstly, keep-up interventions are intended to assist learners who require help in reinforcing and enhancing their knowledge so that the risk of falling behind can be lessened; catch-up interventions are implemented for learners who have already fallen behind and the gaps in their understanding have resulted in them being unable to make more progress within a particular aspect of the curriculum. For both interventions to be put into action, assessment is key, and this is where a teacher's knowledge of the learners in their classroom is really important, this goes beyond specific academic needs and should be holistic in approach, taking into account the wider needs of all learners, including their resilience and their ability to self-regulate whilst recognising their own specific learning needs. Interventions are not just an opportunity to support academic priorities, but also can be applied to all aspects of the visible and non-visible curriculum in school. The way in which interventions are structured with one-to-one or small-group work can be powerful and provide an opportunity to develop reassuring connections with others, both peers and adults alike; this positivity can make a significant impact. Below is a case study to illustrate how a keep-up intervention can support learners to ensure that their needs are responded to in an adaptive way.

CASE STUDY

A Year 6 class were enjoying their unit of work focusing upon Space. During the third lesson the focus of their learning was exploring what solar and lunar eclipses are and the key learning included being able to describe the orbit of the Sun, Moon and Earth – and specifically what occurs when different eclipses take place. Miss Roberts had experience of teaching this lesson and pre-empted a number of misconceptions, including the children being unclear on orbits – specifically the way in which the Moon and Earth rotate around the Sun. Previously, the children had created models to demonstrate this phenomenon and Miss Roberts had noted those learners who were still unsure of the concept. She also focused upon their responses when discussion took place with talking partners on the carpet to inform her assessment of their understanding in that lesson. The observation from the start of this lesson and previous formative marking provided her with an insight into those children who needed further support; they were then invited to sit together on the teacher-focus table. As the children individually created a poster to demonstrate how solar and lunar eclipses occur, Miss Roberts live-marked work and was able to offer support in the moment as they worked, recapping key ideas and reinforcing teaching points from the whole-class teaching session. Being able to assess formatively in the lesson so that intervention support was offered in the moment allowed her to respond and adapt appropriately. This approach also means that it is not always the same children who receive direct support; rather, it is a response to need specific to that lesson.

REFLECTIVE ACTIVITY

How do you embed in the moment and responsive teaching into your daily classroom routine when considering interventions?

How do you use assessment, both formally and informally, to inform active interventions that you employ? (Referring back to Chapter 2, Assessment, may be helpful here.)

The next lesson in this sequence was looking specifically at the solar system. How would this keep-up intervention ensure that the risk of the children falling behind is reduced in future lessons?

CATCH-UP INTERVENTIONS

A catch-up intervention can provide support for a specific skill – for example, a reading recovery programme which is focused upon improving progress in reading in terms of fluency and comprehension over a fixed period and with a comprehensive and progressive structure to be followed. Learners would usually be identified following assessments, and these sessions could be arranged as either a one-to-one or small-group intervention.

Another example could be a memory recall intervention to support the needs of a dyslexic learner; again, this would be structured and would link into their targeted support plan. However, it is important to recognise that it is not only those children who are identified as SEN or that have an education, health and care plan (EHCP) that would receive such intervention. As Garry suggests (2020), interventions should respond to the needs of all learners, regardless of individual need. Catch-up interventions often take place whilst a different learning focus is ongoing in the classroom. For example, if a maths assessment had been completed and a group of children were identified as having a gap in their knowledge linked to written methods of division, the learners could be taken out of the classroom so that they could revisit the concepts that they are not secure with and be given the opportunity for more intensive teaching linked to the methods of calculation whilst the rest of the class develop their understanding further.

In this scenario, there are several points to consider.

1. If many of the pupils struggled with this concept in their assessment, this most likely indicates that the teaching approach used initially was not effective and that the focus should be revisited for all learners in the class.

2. The gap between those children who remain in the class and those who are taken out of the lesson to receive a focused intervention will invariably become greater; this is the professional dilemma and moral conundrum for teachers to contemplate when planning and implementing any kind of intervention for their learners. Here, it is the responsibility of the teacher to manage this, thinking carefully about the approach taken.

3. Finally, thought must be given to the way in which teaching is revisited within a catch-up intervention; this is where creativity and a secure pedagogical subject knowledge is essential. In other words, if the way in which the concept was taught for these specific learners initially was not successful, what can be implemented to make sure that, this time, the learning is successfully embedded? As mentioned previously, those practitioners who embrace adaptation and inclusion are often well versed in different methods of teaching, including the use of ICT and other resources to enrich the learning experience – such as multisensory learning and other scaffolds.

AN INTERVENTION TO LIMIT THE NEED FOR FUTURE INTERVENTION

One intervention approach that could result in it being less likely for a child to require a catch-up intervention is the use of pre-teaching. As a concept, pre-teaching focuses upon certain skills, often linked to imparting key vocabulary, technical concepts and particular knowledge before a sequence is taught – essentially preparing learners and equipping them to tackle new ideas with confidence ahead of the lesson.

CASE STUDY

Mr Frith teaches a Year 1 class and, within their geography topic, the children are learning about the similarities and differences between environments. As part of this sequence of lessons, they will be exploring the human and physical features linked to their local coastal town. In preparation for this, Mr Frith has identified a group of learners, some of whom are diagnosed as having processing difficulties, to spend fifteen minutes with Miss Plant, the class teaching assistant, to introduce them to key vocabulary in preparation ahead of the next geography lesson so that language will not be a barrier for their acquisition of new geographical knowledge. A *word mat* has been created with key phrases from the topic, including mountain, hill, river and valley; there are also spaces for the children to add their own key words if they would like, so that they can contribute and demonstrate their own knowledge and understanding. Using a set of photographs that illustrate local features, including the estuary, the children are encouraged to match the words to the pictures; then they watch a short online video clip of their local environment that includes the key phrases already discussed. Miss Plant shares the learning objectives for the next geography lesson and explains to the group that they will be using the photographs and the word mat to write sentences about the different geographical features.

Pre-teaching allows teachers to monitor understanding and to tackle misconceptions; as a strategy it can help to reduce anxiety for learners who may feel overwhelmed and isolated when a new concept or skill is introduced, if the foundations of learning are secure from the outset, outcomes will also be far more positive.

Opportunities for pre-teaching require careful consideration. As with all interventions, a delicate balance needs to be struck to support a learner but not at the cost of missing further time in the classroom or participation in whole-school sessions such as assemblies. Again, this links to the broader philosophy and ethos of the school and its inclusion policy. Pre-teaching can be led by a teaching assistant during class time; it could be arranged as a small-group session during classroom time or could even be a one-to-one session with a teacher. Whoever leads the intervention, the focus here should be intensive teaching, with key concepts being taught and scaffolds such as word mats or step-by-step processes to follow being fixed so that the learner feels supported and more confident in the whole-class lesson.

SUPPORTING THOSE WHO ARE SECURE IN THEIR LEARNING

Interventions should not just be regarded as a teaching approach to support learners who require support to catch up or keep up; teachers should also be aware of the benefits of intensive teaching opportunities for those who are secure in specific learning concepts in their classrooms and the resulting potential benefits. Despite clear guidance from the government, and as previously discussed, schools establish their own philosophy for inclusion and, as part of this, all children should be offered a level of support to stretch and challenge learning and attainment. If you pause and think for a moment about the types of interventions promoted by schools, you probably first think about a group of children being given support like the two models that Garry (2020) proposed, who more likely than not experience barriers to their learning. The focus of the intervention could be driven by targets in an EHCP, such as strategies of support being led by an expert practitioner – for example, the SENCO. However, it is also important to also consider what the potential impact of focused group work could be on higher-attaining learners.

As an opportunity to develop knowledge further, small-group interventions for confident and secure learners are sometimes overlooked. But delivering targeted activities that extend greater-depth pupils can enhance learning and support wellbeing. The National Association for Able Children in Education (NACE) provides excellent resources for supporting children and explores the concept of breadth and depth learning – including low-threshold, high-ceiling tasks (as discussed in Chapter 4, Adaptive environments and experiences). By considering the needs of more secure learners and by rethinking the curriculum so that all children can flourish, it could be argued that increased levels of achievement for all learners could be achieved thanks to high expectations for all.

Several strategies can be employed to support teaching of learning of more secure learners, including careful consideration of the task itself, ensuring that there is adequate challenge and opportunity for the individual to be active in their thinking. Offsetting this with the opportunity to apply learning in a different way is also beneficial rather than the learner progressing too quicky and the gap becoming greater between the children in the class. The concept of providing stretch and challenge for such learners is much more than an extension task at the end of a lesson; an opportunity in a small-group intervention or a one-to-one session could be a discussion of supportive feedback where tools are shared to help a learner move their own understanding forward by using feedback from a particular task, for example. Providing the opportunity for learners to talk about their progress is important; the pressure that some children experience linked to their ability can create a negative experience, including a detrimental impact upon their emotional wellbeing and self-esteem. Relationships that can be forged from small-group working with an adult can have a positive impact upon broader experiences in schools and should not be undervalued or overlooked.

REFLECTIVE ACTIVITY

Have you seen interventions for secure learners in school? If so, what was the impact for these learners?

Consider how support for secure learners can be implemented so that the activities are more adaptive and less differentiated in approach. How can more breadth and depth of learning be facilitated rather than simply moving learning on more quickly?

TEACHING ASSISTANTS

Workforce numbers in England demonstrate the government's commitment to supporting teacher workload and the inclusion of more children in mainstream education. According to the *School Workforce in England* data (National Statistics, 2023), there are 281,100 full-time employed teaching assistants; this is an increase of 5,300 members of staff since 2021 and an overall increase of 59,600 since 2011, when the census was introduced. Historically, teaching assistants have been used as an active participant in lessons, monitoring and supporting as required, taking responsibility for some teaching activities and working with specific groups – often, those learners who are struggling to keep up or who have gaps in their knowledge as identified by Garry (2020).

The EEF's *Making the Best Use of Teaching Assistants: Guidance Report* (2021) highlights how teaching assistants are sometimes regarded as an informal resource for those children at most need and their support is often provided outside the classroom – for example, in a corridor or library space rather than in an inclusive capacity within the class environment. Here, the gap can become significantly greater between those children in the classroom and those who are segregated and working outside. The report makes the case that teaching assistants should be encouraged to add value to the work of a teacher, rather than simply replacing them, and that schools should ensure that all children have equal time to work in the classroom with their teacher. Any interventions should be linked to the classroom learning and be planned and structured robustly with clear learning objectives so that if the intervention group is being taught outside the classroom, the children can be reintegrated back easily at any point in the learning sequence.

As part of the toolkit of intervention approaches, whoever delivers the activities needs to understand the needs of each learner as an individual so that support can be optimised and tailored to suit specific needs – whether it is an intervention to support emotional and social needs for a recently bereaved child, an in-the-moment classroom intervention to support knowledge for a learner who is struggling to calculate using a specific strategy, or a longer programme of intervention to support reading recovery, they must be confident in the intended outcomes of the activity and have the skills and knowledge to be able to support effectively. It is the responsibility of the classroom teacher to ensure that, if a teaching assistant is used to lead an intervention of any type, they have the skills and are best placed to be employed for a specific focus.

CASE STUDY

Miss Sanghera has a Year 4 class which includes several children who are struggling to retain their multiplication facts and lack fluency in their recall; this is causing some concern as the statutory multiplication tables check (MTC) will be completed later in the year. After the first pupil progress meeting in October, the headteacher and maths subject lead in conjunction with Miss Sanghera have identified five children who will be supported with their multiplication tables knowledge over a period of ten weeks in a small-group intervention, led by the class teaching assistant, Mr Simpson. A programme has been devised by the maths subject lead and will include different activities to build fluency, including IT resources and games, practical activities and homework tasks. When designing the intervention, the colleagues consider the following key questions.

- How have assessment outcomes been shared with the member of staff so they know why this child is being chosen for an intervention? (This could be after formative assessment including questioning, observation, pupil progress meetings or summative feedback after a test, for example.)

- Does Mr Simpson have the knowledge and skills to support and develop and adapt the intervention appropriately? What specific training needs to be identified as a requirement and also to be provided so that the intervention can be carried out successfully?

- How is time allocated so that discussions can take place between Miss Sanghera and Mr Simpson before or after the sessions to share updates on progress and next steps?

- How can the learning that is taking place during the intervention be woven back into class sessions and how can any gaps in learning be addressed in terms of lost learning time during the intervention session and the children who remain in the classroom?

- Where and when is the intervention taking place? Will the session be scheduled in lesson time? If so, which curriculum subject will be affected, and will this be taken into consideration?

- Is time being prioritised so that the intervention can take place regularly – what could be potential reasons as to why Mr Simpson is unable to lead the intervention and how can this be mitigated by Miss Sanghera (other demands on his time, break duty, staff cover etc.)?

SUPPORTIVE PARTNERSHIPS THROUGH INTERVENTIONS

As with all elements of school life, effective partnerships with all stakeholders are essential to provide the very best support for learners, particularly those with more complex needs. It is also important to ensure that positive relationships are encouraged and sustained between the school and families, where all viewpoints are considered, respected and valued. Many outside agencies contribute to the package of interventions that are provided in school, including *virtual schools* for looked after children, speech and language therapists and CAMHS, to mention just a few. Schools should prioritise protected time for teachers and teaching assistants to liaise with external colleagues to ensure that the correct support is in place, sharing their expert knowledge of best practice and, crucially, their understanding of the specific requirements of the learner. The *SEND Code of Practice* (DfE, 2015) highlights the need for children and parents to be included in decision-making at all levels and schools should ensure that this is evident within their values and ethos.

As discussed earlier, interventions can be delivered in many ways, from a quick adaptation in the moment – for example, moving a child to work with an adult-led group after live marking has flagged a misconception – to a more structured programme of intervention to support a specific aspect of the curriculum or a personal issue, for example emotional support after a change in personal circumstances. When a child is selected for a longer-term package of intervention, parents and caregivers should be notified of the support that is being given to their child to ensure absolute clarity; communication here is key.

CASE STUDY

Mr Taylor taught a Year 4 class and had recently started an intervention group on Monday and Thursday afternoons, focusing on key facts in maths including times-tables and number bonds. He chose six children from the class to receive extra targeted support for a ten-week block of two 30-minute sessions after assessing the children on their progress. Mr Taylor sent a letter to the children's parents and caregivers to explain why the children had been chosen, the timings of the group and the focus of the sessions – with the learning outcome that the children would become more confident and secure with their knowledge regarding the key number facts. He invited the parents and caregivers to contact him should they wish to discuss the aims of the intervention; he had also had the opportunity to explain to them face to face as a parents' evening had recently taken place. Halfway through the intervention, the parents and caregivers were given an update on progress; he also sent a brief questionnaire asking questions linked to their observations of the children's confidence and progress with the key skills. Some parents asked if they could help to consolidate their child's understanding, so Mr Taylor provided activities including number games to play at home. At the end of the ten-week block, a summary was shared with the families.

The way in which Mr Taylor communicated with the families was open and responsive; he ensured that they understood the intent of the intervention, the journey that their child was following in terms of their learning and the individual impact of the support. As a result, the parents and caregivers felt included and valued – indeed, empowered to support at home. They had a voice.

REFLECTIVE ACTIVITY

- If Mr Taylor had not communicated in this way, how do you think some families would have felt if their child came home and said that they were having help twice a week but were unable to articulate what the support was?

- Is it possible to manage communication with families whilst balancing a challenging workload? How can parents be given a voice?

- Reflect upon how careful communication can mitigate wider issues. Can you think of further examples of practice that you have observed that have managed this successfully?

OVERCOMING THE CHALLENGES OF INTERVENTIONS

Despite the benefits of interventions, there are several potential barriers that must be considered to ensure that support put in place is effective and does not negatively impact other aspects of the overall learning experience. As demonstrated in the case study above, careful thought must be given to the quality of staffing provision, particularly for longer-term, catch-up interventions. It is the responsibility of the school leadership and the class teachers to ensure that all staff involved in any activity, whether academic or more holistic, are trained effectively so that they can provide the highest-quality support possible. In some cases it may be more appropriate for a qualified teacher or the SENCO to lead the intervention group.

Strict scheduling is necessary to ensure consistency in the sessions. Schools are busy places and staff have to be adaptable to respond to in-the-moment requests for their time, especially teaching assistants who may be required to provide cover for an absent teacher, or even help with emergency medical cover for a poorly child. This can lead to a loss of time in an intervention and can sometimes mean that a session is cancelled or postponed. Although such situations can be difficult to avoid, it is important to reflect upon the impact that this could have on self-esteem of the learners in the group, especially if this becomes a frequent issue.

Some children may be supported in more than one intervention over the period of a week. An example could be an autistic child who has support in the mornings with a teaching assistant for reading comprehension; often is supported by the class teacher for in-the-moment guided group work; has pre-teaching sessions for foundation subjects in the afternoon; and then twice a week goes to the sensory room for positive play sessions focusing specifically on their social and emotional needs. Responding to the EHCP for this child, the school has been adept at providing robust support. However, it would be easy to acknowledge how the child could easily feel overwhelmed with the number of one-to-one and small-group interventions. Anyone who has worked with a learner in a one-to-one situation will know how intense this way of working is; there is nowhere for the child to 'hide' – they are the focus of the session and this must be managed to avoid cognitive overload. Of course, whilst this provision is in place, the learner in this scenario is being taken out of their classroom environment and missing out on other core areas of learning. Unfortunately, children are not given the same opportunities to experience the full curriculum as catch-up sessions in maths and English are sometimes prioritised over foundation subjects including primary foreign languages, PE and music. This can be frustrating and lead to a sense of isolation and a lack of identity, particularly when learners who struggle academically are often those who enjoy physical activities and often excel in creative-based activities. If possible, flexibility in the timetable can help here, although this is not always easily accomplished due to the rigid nature of the curriculum and the fast pace of a learning sequence. Balancing support whilst meeting the needs of all learners in the most efficient way is a true ethical dilemma for teachers and school leaders. If adaptive and responsive interventions are employed within the classroom, including carefully scaffolded learning and flexible groupings as a first step, some of the challenges outlined here could be potentially minimised as the need for focused one-to-one is reduced with quality-first, adaptive teaching strategies.

MONITORING AND ASSESSING

Monitoring is an important aspect of the implementation of any intervention; the intended learning outcomes should be a thread that runs throughout each session and careful assessment should be carried out to decide how a programme of support should be delivered before the intervention begins. When a teacher reacts in the moment during a lesson – flexibly moving children's groups as a response to their participation or performance at the start of a lesson, for example – assessment is the catalyst, and the adaptation is the driver of the response.

An effective intervention can be created to support the specific needs of a child or a group of children. This could be a package of support in addition to the classroom diet or an adaption of materials as discussed earlier in this chapter; however, regardless of how the intervention is established, practitioners must reflect upon the initial intent and impact of their provision to ensure that it is making a positive difference to the learner. The EEF (2021) suggests that an intervention programme should be timetabled regularly (three to five days a week) and delivered during a timescale of between eight and twenty weeks so that adequate time is given to demonstrate impact.

Teachers must provide robust approaches to monitoring progress; this must be considered for all individual learners and be adapted as required whilst ensuring that the activities link to the curriculum of the school. According to the *SEND Code of Practice* (DfE, 2015, p. 99), 'Teachers are responsible and accountable for the progress and development of the pupils in their class, including where pupils access support from teaching assistants or specialist staff.' Teachers must ensure that monitoring systems are efficient and inform next steps; this can be a challenge if someone else is leading the intervention, but it is imperative that this is managed effectively. If a teaching assistant is taking a group into the library, for example, to provide extra support in phonics, the teacher needs to understand what progress is resulting so that adaptions can be made to the planning of the sessions – despite the children not being in the classroom at that time. Good communication is essential between staff. Realistically, this can be a challenge due to the everyday demands in the classroom; however, monitoring progress and ensuring that all staff are aware of progress should not be underestimated. This does not have to be an onerous task; planning could be annotated with notes from the lesson and shared with the teacher, or a simple red, amber and green rating tick list to show progress towards a learning outcome would provide a simple overview. All members of staff involved in the delivery of interventions should be trained so that they can provide effective support. The EEF (2021) suggests an extensive package of between five and 30 hours of training; this should include assessment guidance and how to respond to need. The key message here is that if a child or a group of learners are being taken out for intensive support away from the classroom and being supported by another member of staff that is not the class teacher, their progress is still the responsibility of the class teacher.

This diagram highlights the importance of assessment throughout the intervention process – not just at the beginning where learners are identified, although this is an important part of the cycle. When planning a targeted response, consideration should be given to the learner's existing knowledge and understanding as this will help them to identify links in their learning and consolidate understanding. Adaptation is a thread that runs through the cycle whilst being mindful of the intended learning outcomes; a balance of informal observation and careful questioning can inform next steps and help staff respond to need as required.

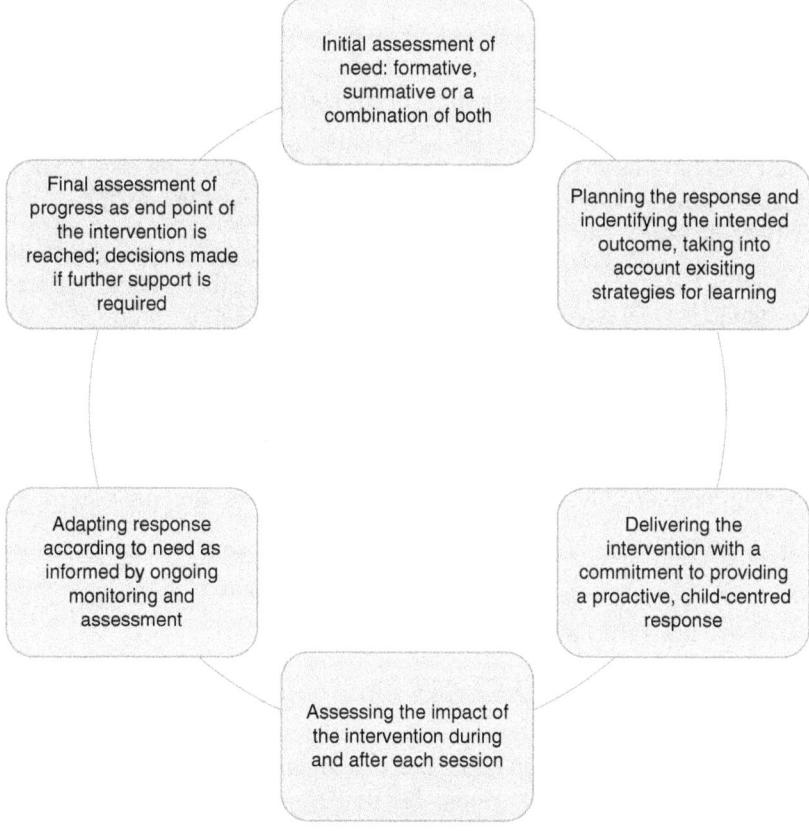

Figure 6.1   Ongoing adaptive intervention assessment cycle

FINAL THOUGHTS

Regardless of the intervention's focus – be it academic or taking into consideration a more holistic approach, including support for social, emotional or behavioural needs so that in the long term a learner is more able to access the curriculum successfully – as a practitioner you must plan with impact and intent in mind. As part of the process, links to wider learning must be prioritised so that the children can see links to their classroom learning and to the wider values of the school if they are being removed from the classroom to complete specific tasks. As with all adaptive considerations, personalising provision is an essential ingredient; as discussed in this chapter, pre-teaching can be one way of reducing the need for more formal interventions, along with carefully modelled teaching (as discussed in Chapter 5, Scaffolding). Finally, consideration must be given to the workload of staff, including that of teaching assistants, as a team; recognise individuals' strengths and how these can be best used to support learning. Do not underestimate the intensity of working one-to-one and in small groups for the facilitator and the learners alike; collaborate in order to refine practice and reflect upon future progress.

REFLECTIVE ACTIVITY

Think about any intervention implemented in your setting that has been led by an adult – this could have been you taking the lead, it could have been a teacher assistant led by you or you could have been leading an activity planned by someone else. If possible, you could observe a colleague in practice as they lead an intervention session. The intervention activity could have a catch-up or keep-up focus.

Make a list of the benefits for the learners and the challenges that you have reflected upon when considering this intervention in more depth. Are the limitations practical - for example, timetabling issues or the location of the group work - or are they more deeply rooted - for example, the expertise of the facilitator or the complexity of the needs of the learners?

Highlight good practice: are the children clear on the expectations of their intervention? If this is a programme of intervention, are the children aware of the 'end point' to which they are working towards? Are there links between the support and the classroom focus?

Consider how any limitations could be overcome. Is there a simple fix for these issues?

How robustly do you think that a monitoring cycle was reinforced during this intervention, and do you think it was truly adaptive?

How was the inclusive strategy of the school and its ethos towards inclusion supported by this intervention?

Do you think that this intervention had a positive impact upon learning and progress? If yes, how do you know? If no, what would you do differently to ensure a greater level of success in the future?

━━ **KEY TAKEAWAYS** ━━━━━━━━━━━━━━━━━━━━━━━━━━━━━━━━━━━

- Personalise interventions and see them as part of responsive and adaptive teaching.

- Think about the wider impact upon a learner beyond the academic.

- Embed assessment rigorously into any intervention.

- Do not underestimate the importance of partnerships and collaborative working.

FURTHER READING AND RESOURCES

EEF (2018c) *Working with Parents to Support Children's Learning: Guidance Report.* Available at: https://educationendowmentfoundation.org.uk/education-evidence/guidance-reports/supporting-parents

EEF (2021) *Making the Best Use of Teaching Assistants: Guidance Report.* Available at: https://educationendowmentfoundation.org.uk/education-evidence/guidance-reports/teaching-assistants

Webster, R., Bosanquet, P., Franklin, S. and Parker, M. (2021) *Maximising the Impact of Teaching Assistants in Primary Schools: A Practical Guide for School Leaders.* Abingdon: Taylor & Francis.

National Association for Able Children in Education. www.nace.co.uk

Education Endowment Foundation (2018) Making the Best Use of Teaching Assistants. Available at: https://educationendowmentfoundation.org.uk/education-evidence/guidance-reports/teaching-assistants

7

COGNITION AND METACOGNITION

┌─── **CHAPTER OBJECTIVES** ──────────────────────────────────┐

After engaging with this chapter, you will be able to:

- understand what cognition and metacognition is and the difference between them;
- understand the how metacognition is implicit in educational practice;
- be able to apply principles of metacognition to your own practice of adaptive teaching;
- consider and use metacognitive strategies for teaching and assessing in an adaptive environment.

└──┘

INTRODUCTION

If you have had any involvement with education, you will probably have heard of some of these terms: cognition, metacognition, cognitive architecture. John H. Flavell (1928–present), an American developmental psychologist, is most notably credited with developing the concept of *metacognition* in the areas of cognitive psychology and educational psychology. He stated that young children are often quite unaware and limited in their knowledge of how they function cognitively, and often they do little monitoring of their own memory or comprehension of thinking activities. We can think of cognition and metacognition as these two things:

1. *cognitions* are the things we do with our cognitive architecture such as rehearsing, critical thinking and summarising information;

2. *metacognitions* are the strategies we use to monitor these things such as self-assessment, reflection and goal-setting.

We can therefore understand the importance of these concepts when thinking about learners in our classroom and also about adapting our learning and teaching to these individuals. Cognition concerns the mental processes and techniques that learners use to acquire, organise, remember and use information at different times, in different contexts and ways. As teachers, we can therefore see that having knowledge of these areas is absolutely crucial.

Arriving at a definite definition of metacognition is complex, but Flavell (1979) offers the following:

> *Metacognitive knowledge is one's stored knowledge or beliefs about oneself and others as cognitive agents, about tasks, about actions or strategies, and about how all these interact to affect the outcomes of any sort of intellectual enterprise. Metacognitive experiences are conscious cognitive or affective experiences that occur during the enterprise and concern any aspect of it – often, how well it is going.*

(p. 906)

We can think of this in practical terms by considering a learner in a class called Dylan. Dylan is using cognitive and metacognitive strategies which are exemplified below.

- *Cognitive* – Dylan knows he needs to use summarising as a skill, not only for the learning he is completing in class, but also as a general skill for life. He has learnt that he needs to reflect and use metacognitive strategies to help him master this skill. He decides to make a plan of how he will do this, but needs to collect some more information first. Dylan can then engage in cognitive monitoring or metacognition, by doing one or more of the things below which Flavell (1979) described.

- *Metacognitive knowledge* – this is how Dylan thinks and believes that certain actions affect the outcome of his cognitive activity or summarising. For example, if Dylan is trying to improve his summarising in class, he can use a range of factors to help him evaluate how effectively he is achieving this.

- *Person* – Dylan might feel he is very good or very poor at this task of summarising, which may affect his ability to do this, as well as strategies he will select and implement. As such he will use this knowledge to inform other aspects of his metacognitive approach.

- *Task* – Dylan acknowledges and becomes familiar with the task of summarising. Using this information will enable him to select and use certain strategies more effectively.

- *Strategy* – Dylan considers what are the best strategies to ensure he is successful in becoming more effective in summarising information in a lesson. This could be goal-setting or self-reflection on how well he has done or simply seeking the advice of other peers to overcome cognitive bias.

- *Metacognitive experiences* – these are very important for Dylan and often appear when he is engaging in the task of summarising itself. His feelings about that task and his progress have an impact on this process. They are important for several reasons. Firstly, Dylan uses his experiences to create new goals, revise ones that he has already decided upon and to abandon others that are seemingly ineffective. Secondly, these experiences can help Dylan reevaluate his metacognitive knowledge. For example, he might reconsider his understanding of himself as a person, starting to believe he is actually better or worse than he thought at summarising information. He may reconsider the task itself, how complex or simple it is. He may also reconsider how effective the metacognitive strategies he had selected for the task are. Therefore, meta-cognitive experiences are crucial because they could cause Dylan to activate further strategies that lead to two outcomes: improved cognitive function or more efficient metacognitive selection and use.

This chapter will help us to consider these ideas in the context of education, learning and teaching and, especially, adaptive practice. Whilst these are applicable to many areas of education, we begin by talking about metacognition in particular in relation to policy, ped-agogy and, finally, assessment, with a focus on how teachers can continue to respond to individual learning needs and adapt learning and teaching.

━ REFLECTIVE ACTIVITY ━━━━━━━━━━━━━━━━━━━━━━━━━━━━━━━━━

Pick two learners in your class. Considering what we have learnt about cognition and metacognition, answer the following questions.

What differences and similarities do you notice in the way these two learners differ in their cognition?

How do these two learners differ in their confidence in themselves as a learner? Do they have different views of how successful they are as a student in your class?

What similarities or differences in task success do you notice? For example, what tasks do they find easy to do and what do they find more challenging? Is one learner better at remembering than the other?

Consider the different ways in which these learners approach learning and teaching. How are they different or the same?

Based on these reflections, create an individualised plan of how you might support and challenge these learners in your classroom. Might you attempt to encourage them to think differently about themselves as a learner?

━ REFLECTIVE ACTIVITY ━━━━━━━━━━━━━━━━━━━━━━━━━━━━━━━━━

After reading this section regarding metacognition and policy, have a professional dis-cussion with a member of your school or university teaching team. Some points to discuss are:

- how important is knowledge of cognition and metacognition in the curriculum?

- how do they feel knowledge of metacognition and metacognitive strategies are embedded in the day-to-day practices of their institutions?

- what improvements could be made to ensure metacognitive practices and strategies are more effectively used to produce better outcomes for all involved?

COGNITION AND METACOGNITION IN POLICY

Whilst the DfE only explicitly mentions metacognition in the ECF (2019a) for BTs in 'Standard 4 – Plan and teach well structured lessons', we argue that teachers must be aware that knowledge of cognition and metacognition is essential for adaptive teaching implicitly throughout the ECF and *Teachers' Standards* (DfE, 2021). ECF Standard 4 (as above) states that BTs should:

Learn that …

5. *Explicitly teaching pupils metacognitive strategies linked to subject knowledge, including how to plan, monitor and evaluate, supports independence and academic success.*

Learn how to …

Plan effective lessons, by:

- *Breaking tasks down into constituent components when first setting up independent practice (e.g. using tasks that scaffold pupils through metacognitive and procedural processes).*

In Ofsted's (2021) *Principles Behind Ofsted's Research Reviews and Subject Reports* it acknowledges the huge increase in study of cognitive science and the impact this has had on understanding how students learn. It suggests this has informed its *Education Inspection Framework* (Ofsted, 2023a). Although Ofsted does not mention metacognition and only mentions cognition once in the latter publication, it will become clear that metacognition is especially important when considering learning and adapting our pedagogical and assessment practices. In relation to metacognition, and considering the discussion above, we feel that metacognition has a huge part to play, especially in Standard 5: 'Adapt teaching' (DfE, 2019a). Some important points from Standard 5 to consider are:

- *Pupils learn at different rates and need different support.* Understanding cognition and metacognitive strategies can help us, as teachers, understand why different students process and learn information in different ways and at different rates. Because the cognitive functioning of these students can differ so much, it is likely we need to understand this and adapt our pedagogical and assessment practices effectively. For example, we may need to reduce the amount of information we supply to learners to avoid overloading them cognitively. Alternatively, through our ongoing formative assessment, we may realise that a learner is finding a task more challenging cognitively, so we adapt the way we supply this information. As such we can adapt our strategies based on this understanding.

- *We need to understand pupils' differences such as their prior knowledge and their barrier to learning.* Similarly to above, we need to explore the ways in which barriers to learning for specific pupils may manifest in the classroom. Getting learners to use metacognitive strategies can help us to understand these barriers and adapt our practices accordingly. For example, we may expect our learners to be able to chunk information down into a smaller, more manageable information. However, due to the complexity of this process some may find this incredibly difficult. Others may have limited prior knowledge due to various factors such as large absence from school, as was seen during the Covid-19 pandemic. Acknowledging gaps in prior knowledge, as well as metacognitive experiences, can help us plan and respond to learner needs more effectively.

- *By understanding these points we can provide targeted support in a responsive and adaptive way.* As discussed in the example of Dylan, by understanding learners' cognitive abilities and their metacognitive knowledge and experiences, we can tailor not only what we will teach and how we will teach it but also how we can help a learner to develop goals and aspirations for themselves. It is likely that by creating a culture of continuous growth and improvement, by utilising metacognitive strategies, learners will develop more positive attitudes to their own personal growth and development. Greater self-reflection, not only on the part of the teacher but also by learners, will ensure they reflect on their own learning and their successes and limitations in that process.

Finally, by ensuring metacognition is not forgotten in policy, we can ensure that it is enacted in practice. Raising expectations, motivation and improving the learning culture are all outcomes that come from ensuring metacognitive awareness is built into any effective learning environment. Now we will think about how metacognitive awareness can be built into our pedagogical knowledge and practice.

METACOGNITION AS PEDAGOGIC STRATEGY

It is not necessarily clear how metacognition and pedagogy can be united to bring about some of the benefits already discussed. It is less clear from our experience of working with teachers in schools how metacognition and adaptive learning and teaching might be realised. Look at the following case study which focuses on using metacognition in the classroom as an explicit pedagogic strategy.

━━ **CASE STUDY** ━━━

Ms Rodriguez, a very experienced mathematics teacher, recognised the need to enhance her students' learning experiences by incorporating metacognitive strategies into her pedagogical approach. She has been trialling this and plans the following lesson which contains some metacognitive strategies:

- *Introduction (five minutes)*

She begins by engaging and activating prior knowledge, asking learners to reflect on the previous lesson with questions such as:

- o what exactly did we learn in the lesson?

- o how well do you think you learnt this knowledge/concept/skill?

- o what went well in this lesson?

- o what was difficult for you?

- o what changes could you make to your learning approach today?

She then asks the learners to discuss these questions with a peer on their mixed-ability table. After this she encourages learners to share their reflections with the whole class.

- *Aim setting (five minutes)*

Ms Rodriguez asks the learners to set a goal for what they want to achieve today in the lesson. This should be based on what they learnt from their discussion in the previous lesson.

- *Explicit learning and modelling (twenty minutes)*

Moving onto new learning material, Ms Rodriguez uses a range of pedagogical strategies to encourage her learners. She uses a step-by-step worked example of what they will be doing in the lesson. As well as this, she uses a range of high-quality questioning to ensure she knows what students have learnt. Dialogue is essential and she builds in lots of opportunities for learners to discuss and gain feedback on their thinking. Equally she has ensured there is a range of representations so that the cognitive overload for students is not too great.

- *Independent practice with ongoing formative assessment (twenty minutes)*

With worked examples available on the working wall and a wealth of guided practice, learners continue their exploration by engaging in learning experiences independently and with their groups. They focus on their own individual learning goals, as set at the

(Continued)

(Continued)

beginning of the lesson, choosing materials which are helpful to them, managing their time effectively. Throughout this independent learning time, the teacher encourages the learners to reflect on their progress.

Throughout the independent phase the teacher and other adults in the classroom move around the room, homing in on specific learners who they know, from previous assessment for learning, may need some extra support or scaffolding.

- *Peer assessment and reflection (five minutes)*

Learners share what they have done with their peers and discuss the progress they have made in relation to the targets they set at the beginning of the lesson. They consider how successful they think they have been.

- *Whole-class reflection (five minutes)*

The class is encouraged to come together to discuss the learning as a community and share their own reflections of how successful they have been in the learning process.

REFLECTIVE ACTIVITY

Now you have explored the case above, consider if and how Ms Rodriguez is utilising metacognitive strategies and thinking in her learning and teaching philosophy. Especially, consider how the learners are being encouraged to think about their own learning and how this relates to their metacognitive knowledge of themselves, their task and their strategies.

BUILDING METACOGNITION INTO YOUR LEARNING AND TEACHING

Tarrant and Holt (2016) suggest that it is important to develop structures which can scaffold and support the kinds of metacognitive activity that we have discussed so far. A big misconception about metacognition, especially in relation to learning and teaching, is that it will happen spontaneously and naturally as learners develop cognitively over time. However, whilst this may or may not be true, as teachers we can certainly encourage our learners to develop this important skill. It is essential for academic success but also for life in general that learners begin this process of reflecting on their cognitive success. We can support this process through a selection of pedagogical strategies or practices highlighted below, some of which have been explored above in the lesson taught by Ms Rodriguez. Here are some others which can also be easily included in your pedagogic strategies. You may be using some of them in your learning and teaching already.

SETTING CLEAR LEARNING GOALS AND EXPECTATIONS

One simple way we can and often do encourage reflection and metacognition in our classrooms is by giving our learners clear and accessible learning goals and outcomes. These are usually linked to the national curriculum and consist of knowledge or skills we want our learners to master in a lesson. Alternatively, it could be smaller steps that we want our learners to take on the path to achieving larger outcomes. However, what is less common is asking learners to create their own learning goals or outcomes for a lesson. Whilst this may seem like more work and may be more difficult, as with anything, it is all about familiarity and encouraging learners to become used to this practice in their day-to-day routines. This could be something simple and could be aligned to the three areas of metacognitive knowledge discussed above. You could focus on asking learners to generate a goal focused on themselves as a learner, the learning they are engaging in or the strategy they are using. For example, let's imagine Ben is a learner in your class who finds getting questions wrong very difficult. You want him to create a goal for the lesson so he can shift this focus on always being correct. He could create a goal focusing on becoming more positive about himself as a learner if he finds something difficult or gets something wrong. Equally, we could encourage Ben to create a goal focusing on choosing tasks which encourage him to attempt tasks which are more challenging or do not necessarily always result in being right or wrong. Finally, we could encourage him to choose a goal which focuses on a strategy to help him do this, such as being more holistic and realistic in his approach to learning. Regardless of the focus, we can see a shift away from the teacher owning learning to learners taking ownership of their successes. More importantly, all of this activity allows for the teacher to adapt their approach to the learning as they become more aware of these factors of the learner's cognitive profile.

CREATE TIME FOR METACOGNITIVE EXPERIENCES

It may sound simple, but creating time in your lessons for metacognitive experiences can be really important if you want to include this into your practice. Without giving time for this activity and embedding it into learners' everyday routine it will not happen. It may be that you are already using some time at the end of your lessons to reflect on the learning that has taken place. Plenaries and reflections have become a common segment of most learning and teaching sessions. This is a great opportunity to make a slight swift towards encouraging reflecting not only on the learning, but also on the cognitive progress of learning itself. You could explore the successes and shortcomings of the learning. For example, you could simply ask learners to reflect on what was easy or difficult in the lesson for them. As we shall discuss later in the chapter, this will provide you with a wealth of assessment information that can be used for planning future learning experiences.

METACOGNITIVE MODELLING

Metacognitive modelling is crucial if we want to ensure our learners begin and become proficient in metacognitive processes. As with any aspect of learning, explicitly modelling what we want our learners to do is crucial. As previously argued, we cannot guarantee they will engage in this process through osmosis, simply because others around them are. A thinking-out-loud process is essential when engaging in this kind of pedagogic strategy because it is a process that necessarily takes place in the head. For example, a teacher may notice that their learners are engaging in an activity and using a strategy or method that is ineffective. As such, they may want to draw their learners' attention to this by encouraging them to reflect on the efficacy of this process. They can narrate this out loud, providing a worked example of the thinking process. Another aspect of this process is inducting your learners into a new set of vocabulary, almost a new language of metacognition. As we shall discuss next, modelling the kinds of language and how it can be used in learning is a great way of explicitly teaching metacognition. Of course, we need to make sure the language we are using is appropriate for our learners and, if not, we should adapt it accordingly. Below you will find some examples of language that can be helpful for learners.

METACOGNITION TALK

Metacognition is accompanied by a whole range of language which is appropriate. You yourself may have found some of the vocabulary used in this chapter new and, at times, quite overwhelming. Using this experience, we can place ourselves in the shoes of our learners. Therefore, scaffolding metacognitive language is important because, as we have discussed, we need to adapt our language for the cognitive level of our learners. Using language that is overly abstract and complicated will likely create barriers for our learners and create a negative experience of the process. Engaging with learners in a stage-appropriate manner will be crucial. For example, consider the below interaction between a KS1 learner and their teacher:

> *Mr Ahmed*: Good morning, Freda! How are you feeling about our maths lesson today?
>
> *Freda*: Hi, Mr Ahmed! I'm feeling OK, but sometimes I get a little stuck when there are too many numbers.
>
> *Mr Ahmed*: I appreciate your honesty, Freda. Let's work together to make sense of it. Can you tell me, what do you usually use when numbers start to feel tricky?
>
> *Freda*: Well, sometimes I count on my fingers, but I know that's not always the best way.
>
> *Mr Ahmed*: That's a great start! Counting on fingers can help, but let's think about other strategies too. How about we try using pictures or drawings to represent the numbers? Would that make it easier for you?
>
> *Freda*: Yeah, I like drawing! I think this may help me.

The language used encourages Freda to think about what is tricky and how certain strategies might help her. Now consider another dialogue between a teacher and an older student and their peer:

Ms Bern: Today, let's take a moment to reflect on our learning. How do you feel about the recent geography topic we completed?

Johan: To be honest it was challenging. I think I learnt a lot but I had to concentrate to organise my ideas and present them effectively.

Ms Bern: Great to hear. It's very important to remain reflective. How about you, Ellie?

Ellie: For me it was the time management. If I had started earlier, I probably would have done better.

Ms Bern: Let's delve deeper into that. Do you think you're a person who manages time well generally? What specific challenges did you face, and how do you think you can improve?

Ellie: I underestimate how long tasks will take and I tend to procrastinate. I need to break projects down into smaller tasks and set realistic deadlines.

Ms Bern: What do you think Johan? Do you have any advice for Ellie on how she might improve this skill? Do you think breaking down tasks can make them more manageable?

Johan: Yes, I think it can. For example, when completing my maths homework, I set a timer, so I know exactly how much time I have for each question.

Ms Bern: Do you think that helps you remain focused and less overloaded by information? It's important to recognise these challenges and actively work on strategies to overcome them. Now, both of you, how do you think this project has contributed to your overall learning and development?

Throughout the dialogue, both teacher and learners are being asked to reflect on their efficacy in tasks; the dialogue between the learners encourages evaluation of their individual strategies whilst also sharing what other strategies might be useful.

METACOGNITIVE SENTENCE STEMS

Another excellent way of adapting our metacognitive practice is by utilising sentence stems which encourage learners to think more deeply about this practice. By offering sentence stems, which can be displayed around a learning environment for learners to refer to, we can unintentionally instigate this kind of thinking in our learners. Equally, when engaging in learning and teaching, we can also model the use of these metacognitive sentence stems so that others know how they are to be used. Consider the sentence stems given in Table 7.1 for different key stages.

Table 7.1   Sentence stems for different key stages

Types of metacognitive knowledge	Sentence stems to support EYFS/Key Stage 1 pupils	Sentence stems to support Key Stage 2 pupils
About the person as a learner	'I know I am good at learning about ...' 'I know I find it difficult when ...' 'My favourite type of learning involves ...'	'I believe I excel in x because ...' 'I struggle with x because it involves ...' 'When the learning involves x, I really thrive because ...'
About the task they are completing	'Today, I learnt that ...' 'One thing I know more about is ...' 'My confidence has grown in ...'	'I understood the concept better when ...' 'The most important thing I learnt was ...' 'The most challenging part of this task is x because ...'
About the strategy they are using	'I can get better at learning by ...' 'I can break this down into smaller steps by ...' 'I need to pay attention to ...'	'I found that using the strategy of x helped me with ...' 'Next time, I might try a new strategy like x to ...' 'If I come across a similar problem, I would change my strategy to ...'
About setting goals	'For me, doing well in learning looks like ...' 'I aim to succeed at ...' 'This goal is important because ...'	'In this learning session I hope to achieve ...' 'I am open to changing this goal to something different if ...' 'If I come across a similar problem, I would change my strategy to ...'
About emphasising effort	'Even if it's hard, I will keep trying because ...' 'Not getting this quite right will teach me ...' 'I feel proud of myself when I ...'	'If I encounter x, I will ensure I succeed by ...' 'In the face of difficulties, my strategy for learning and improvement will be ...' 'Even if it's hard, I will keep trying because ...'

METACOGNITION AS ASSESSMENT AS LEARNING

In Chapter 2, Assessment, we spent a great deal of time thinking about formative assessment and assessment for learning as a foundational practice for adapting learning and teaching. Here we want to explore the oft-forgotten practice of assessment *as* learning and its relationship with metacognition. In particular, we want to explore how assessment as learning practices, as a type of metacognitive experience, can help to support and develop metacognitive knowledge about ourselves as learners, the learning we are engaging in and the strategies we use to regulate and monitor our successes as well as the efficacy of those strategies. When we encourage our learners to engage in these kinds of practices, we are gaining access to a wide range of assessment information we normally would not. This is also another excellent way for learners to tap into their tacit knowledge (explored in Chapter 2) and for them to make this experience more visible for us. When we think of metacognition as assessment as learning, we can focus this discussion principally around our learners, putting them in the driving seat of this practice. Predominantly, we can do this by encouraging our learners to engage in self-assessment and peer assessment. Self-assessment is especially important for developing our learners' metacognitive knowledge about how they view themselves as learners, the tasks they are engaging in and the strategies they are using. Peer assessment is vital for developing our learners' metacognitive experience so they can adapt and change their metacognitive knowledge appropriately and with efficacy.

SELF-ASSESSMENT AS METACOGNITIVE KNOWLEDGE

There are many ways that we can encourage our learners to start engaging in self-assessment practices. Below are some practical ways that you can begin introducing this practice into your classroom.

PROFORMAS SUCH AS KWL GRIDS

Giving a scaffolded structure is a great way to introduce our learners to the process of self-assessing. One excellent way is a KWL, which encourages learners to think about their prior knowledge, what they want to learn and, finally, to reflect on what they have learnt over a period of time. Easily applied to any subject or curriculum area, learners are assisted in directing their own learning by continually adding to the grid over time and are prompted to reflect on the process of completing the grid. As a teacher, we can also use this grid to assess and reflect on the progress of learners, considering how we might need to adapt our pedagogy or content to help support this process.

Table 7.2   *KWL grid*

What I know (Prior knowledge)	What I want to know (Intended knowledge)	What I have learnt (Enacted knowledge)

REFLECTIVE JOURNAL

Supporting learners to reflect on their own learning also creates greater autonomy and engagement. Asking learners to complete a set of metacognitive questions at the end of a lesson, day or week can easily be built into a learner's timetable. Questions can focus on a range of topics such as goal-setting and acquisition, reflecting on progress towards such goals, identifying strengths and weaknesses.

TRAFFIC LIGHT SYSTEM

A traffic light system is a great way of asking learners to reflect on their level of understanding throughout a lesson and self-assessing. You can make simple resources for your learners such as lolly sticks with different colours or even flashcards. At intervals in your lesson, asking learners to hold up a red, amber or green card, corresponding to how well they are understanding and progressing, can provide invaluable information about the pace of your lesson very quickly. Often it can appear learners are understanding something because they are busy, motivated or simply smiling. However, traffic lights can give learners a medium through which they can show you they need more time to understand something or are confident in what they are learning. These can be adapted to many topics making them versatile for self-assessment.

CREATING YOUR OWN LEARNING OBJECTIVES

We have discussed creating learning objectives as a pedagogic strategy, but they can also be extremely useful for learners when it comes to self-assessment. When a learner has produced a specific goal, this can then be used as a tool for that learner to assess their own success. Asking a learner to reflect on what has gone well during a lesson and how they have progressed towards the goal is important.

CONCEPT MAPS

Concept maps are another excellent tool which can be used metacognitively when learners are self-assessing their understanding and progress. As a graphical tool which usually allows learners to communicate and map different concepts and ideas and their relationship, they are an excellent way for learners to make what they have learnt visible. They are also cognitively less demanding as they focus less on producing large amounts of written information and more on graphically representing key information in ways that make sense for the learner. A learner may, for example, create a concept map of what they have learnt about a topic in history, or the important vocabulary they have learnt in a music lesson. As a self-assessment tool, they can be used by learners to explore their metacognitive knowledge. They can think about how well they have understood something or even reflect on what they think went well or not so well during the learning. Equally, they provide a tool for a teacher to instigate metacognitive experiences in which learners can consider their original goals in relation to their metacognitive knowledge and produce new goals or refine older ones. For teachers they are also an excellent way of seeing what a learner has understood throughout a topic of work.

PEER ASSESSMENT AS METACOGNITIVE EXPERIENCE

Peers can also be an invaluable resource to encourage learners to think more deeply about their cognitive processes. It's likely that many learners use different methods and strategies to help them; these can be shared easily when encouraged. Consider the following dialogue between two learners, Millie and Alfie, which demonstrates a metacognitive experience:

Alfie: Hey, Millie! I've been thinking about our last science assessment. I struggled and I want to figure out how to improve for the next one.

Millie: Yeah, me too, Alfie! What are you thinking of doing differently?

Alfie: Well, I know I didn't plan out how to approach the problems. I want to set some goals for myself before starting the next assignment, so I don't just rush through it.

Millie: What kind of goals are you thinking of? It's a great idea.

Alfie: Maybe making sure to read through the entire question first, breaking it down into smaller steps. I noticed I often get stuck when I try to solve the whole thing at once.

Millie: That sounds like a good plan! I noticed that I tend to rush through without checking my work thoroughly. So, my goal is to slow down and double-check my work before moving on to the next problem.

Alfie: Nice! And I was also thinking of keeping a kind of 'learning journal' where I jot down the strategies that work for me and those that don't. That way, I can look back and see what's been effective. We can discuss what worked and what we can improve on.

Metacognitive discussions offer a great example of how two strategies can be shared when instigated in a learning environment. This discussion provides an example of how peer discussions can allow learners to reflect upon and alter their metacognitive knowledge strategies. It can also be very useful in challenging and overcoming cognitive bias that may be present for some learners in their experiences. Take the following example:

> *Millie:*   Hey, Alfie! I am not sure why we're doing this. It seems like a waste of time.
>
> *Alfie:*   I think it's a great opportunity for us to learn something new and apply what we've learnt!
>
> *Millie:*   It's just another useless task. I'd rather focus on the stuff we already know.
>
> *Alfie:*   I think trying new things helps us grow and improves our understanding. Plus, it's a chance to challenge ourselves.
>
> *Millie:*   That's true, but I just want to focus on things I like learning about and doing. I get better marks and feedback.
>
> *Alfie:*   Yes, but isn't learning about more than just getting good marks? I mean, we're here to expand our knowledge and skills, right? It sounds like you're sticking to what you know and avoiding anything new or different, even if it might be beneficial in the long run.

These conversations can be very beneficial to help learners move or change their thinking in some way. As above, Millie's metacognitive knowledge could be altered by the experience of reflecting on learning with Alfie.

REFLECTIVE ACTIVITY

Consider the following case and make recommendation.

A primary school, a diverse and inclusive place to learn and grow, wants to embark on a journey to enhance student learning and adapt teaching by integrating metacognitive strategies into its learning and teaching strategies. The senior leadership team recognises the importance of cultivating metacognition to empower students with the skills needed for independent and reflective learning.

The challenge

The school faces challenges in ensuring that all students, regardless of their cultural and social background and abilities, can engage meaningfully with the national curriculum. There is a need to adapt teaching methodologies to address individual differences and foster a deeper understanding of content.

Think of recommendations that could be made in the following areas:

- integrating metacognition into lessons plans;
- developing CPD focused on metacognition;
- adapting learning and teaching and assessment practices;
- utilising technology to help support metacognition and adaptive teaching.

Once you have made your list of recommendations, perhaps share and discuss these with an expert teacher or a university mentor. Reflect on how successful you feel these recommendations might be. It could be possible to try one of these recommendations in your school and assess its impact on learners.

FINAL THOUGHTS

This chapter has discussed the important concepts of cognition and metacognition in the context of education, particularly focusing on the ideas put forth by Flavell (1979). It is important to remember when adapting practice that cognition refers to mental processes used by learners to acquire and use information, whilst metacognition involves strategies like self-assessment, reflection and goal-setting to monitor and improve cognitive activities. In the context of education policy, the DfE explicitly mentions metacognition in the ECF (2019a) and acknowledges that cognition and metacognition are crucial for adaptive teaching implicitly throughout the framework and *Teachers' Standards* (2021). Ofsted recognises the impact of cognitive science on understanding how learning takes place, as well as the need for teachers to understand students' varying cognitive differences, adapt pedagogical and assessment practices to those specific differences, and address variations in prior knowledge and barriers to learning. As teachers and senior leaders, it is important to create structures that support metacognitive activity; we suggest embedding pedagogical strategies, such as setting clear learning goals, creating time for metacognitive experiences, metacognitive modelling and using metacognitive language, in everyday learning routines.

KEY TAKEAWAYS

- Whilst metacognition is rarely explicitly mentioned in policy, it is important and has relevance for many teacher activities.
- When adapting learning and teaching it is important to factor in the way children think and how their cognitive abilities may impact on their ability to learn in a certain way and at a certain pace.

(Continued)

(Continued)

- Understanding metacognition and embedding metacognitive activities into your pedagogic strategies can help learners to reflect on their own learning successes and take ownership of their learning.

- Metacognition is crucial when assessing learners as it helps us understand what our students have learnt and how they have gone about doing that.

FURTHER READING AND RESOURCES

EEF (2018) *Metacognition and Self-regulated Learning: Seven Recommendations for Teaching Self-regulated Learning and Metacognition.* Available at: https://d2tic4wvo1iusb.cloudfront.net/eef-guidance-reports/metacognition/EEF_Metacognition_and_self-regulated_learning.pdf

Mulholland, K. (2022) *Voices from the Classroom: Using Worked Examples To Support Pupils' Mathematical Problem-solving.* Available at: https://educationendowmentfoundation.org.uk/news/voices-from-the-classroom-using-worked-examples-to-support-pupils-mathematical-problem-solving

Muncaster, K. and Clarke, S. (2018) *Thinking Classrooms: Metacognition Lessons for Primary Schools.* London: Rising Stars.

8

QUESTIONING

━ CHAPTER OBJECTIVES ━━━━━━━━━━━━━━━━━━━━━━━━━━━━━━━━━━━━━━━

After engaging with this chapter, you will be able to:

- contextualise questioning within adaptive teaching;
- recognise different types of questioning and how these can be used in your classroom;
- recognise different types of responding and how this can be used to give learners autonomy in your learning environment;
- know how you can improve your adaptive questioning and use this to identify misconceptions and address these in learning.

INTRODUCTION

Why do we ask questions? As teachers this is one of the most common activities we engage in and a staple of our assessment practice. Brualdi (1998) suggested that teachers ask as many as 300–400 questions per day, taking up huge segments of teaching time in the classroom. However, as Hattie (2012) has argued, the majority of the questions we ask are simply about recalling facts and activate superficial levels of knowledge. Utilising questioning as a pedagogic tool is much less common in the classroom based on our experience. All too often, very little thought or planning goes into how and why we ask learners questions. We reflect even less on the effectiveness of the questions we are asking which is why our questioning remains ineffective as a practice. Perhaps even more rare, is the idea that we examine how our questioning practices are experienced and reflected upon by our learners. Ask yourself: when was the last time you consulted your learners on how your questioning is perceived or experienced by them?

Sadly, too often our questioning has devolved into a 'game', a game where teachers ask questions relating to what they are thinking, and learners answer by trying to guess this. Considerable amounts of questioning in the classroom have, therefore, become about learners trying to tell teachers what they want to hear and not about being responsive to the ongoing learning in the classroom – and even less about genuine enquiry. This is problematic for several reasons which will be explored in this chapter. Firstly, it has made our use of questioning as an assessment practice hollow and meaningless. If we think back to Chapter 2, Assessment, we discussed the difference between the intended and actual learning taking place in our classrooms. If we just base our questioning on our learning intention and not on what is being learnt, our questioning will not be effective or useful in adapting learning. It means the variety of questioning taking place in the classroom is restricted and misses out on opportunities to genuinely assess the learning and respond to this. Furthermore, it has created a classroom culture which reduces enquiry and conjecture and produces a performative exercise which pretends to be learning. Questioning of this kind is about teaching, not learning.

This chapter tries to remedy this by moving questioning back into the field of learning and away from the activities of teaching; it will explore the relationship between questioning and assessment. Furthermore, it will explore the kinds of questions that are asked commonly in the classroom before considering how adaptive questioning might be fostered, along with adaptive responding. We shall also discuss the concept of misconceptions of bugs in learners' thinking and how questioning, as pedagogy and assessment, can help overcome such limitations in thinking.

LEARNING TO PLAY THE GAME?

There is much good practice taking place in schools; this we cannot deny. However, as Hattie (2012) has argued, lots of teaching taking place in school is superficial as learners attempt to engage in the game of answering questions. We argue this is not learning, but simply a pseudo-activity. It looks like learning, but it isn't because the focus is on the performance of teaching and not learning. Our students are playing the game of answering our questions. Too often assessment and all its associated activities have become a game. Games are not bad per se, but it depends on the type of game our students are engaged in. As Coe (2013) has argued, just because we have taught something does not mean that it has been learnt and we cannot guarantee that our students are actively engaged in the process of learning. We can often fall into the trap, Coe argues, of thinking our students are learning because they are busy, they look engaged and are motivated. Perhaps they are answering questions correctly and the general feeling within the classroom is positive. Yet, again, many of these signs are superficial. Let us take the example of Tim in the case study below.

CASE STUDY

A Year 1 class is engaged in some learning about the Great Fire of London in history. Tim is sat listening carefully and seems to be engaged in the learning. He smiles at the teacher and acknowledges what they are saying. From a distance, it seems like Tim is actively participating in class experiences and completing his work on time. His teacher asks many questions and directs one at Tim. He answers correctly. He raises his hand to answer other questions, nods along during class discussions and completes his work.

It is hard to critique the above example. It seems that Tim is giving us every sign that he is engaging in the learning process and understanding. But, as we mention above, these signs are not necessarily proof that Tim is actively engaged in the learning process and certainly do not prove that he is learning what we intend him to learn. If we consider the goal of questioning to provide answers, then we have transferred our practice into a game of finding the answer; when this has been completed the game ends. This also means thinking has ended. When our learners stop thinking they have stopped learning. If our teaching doesn't encourage learning, then what is the point of it?

We argue that questioning is a great way of getting our learners to think deeply. We shall discuss the pedagogy of asking questions shortly.

Consider the following situation in the classroom:

Teacher: Let's think about this question everyone. What is 10 x 8?

Learner: The answer is 80.

Teacher: Fantastic. Yes, that is correct. Well done.

Later the teacher reflects on this interaction and arrives at the following conclusion:

Teacher: That learner clearly understands this topic because they could answer this question correctly. I think they have grasped multiplying by ten.

On superficial reflection, it seems obvious that the learner understands the concept being learnt because they were able to answer the question correctly. However, if we explore this in more depth, we can ask: what information have we really gained from this questioning interaction? More importantly, how will we use this information to further respond to the needs of the learner? It might be worth pausing for a moment to think deeply about this. What is clear is that when an answer is given correctly, as teachers we make a selection of assumptions. Our learners have 'played the game' and produced what we have asked them to. This also makes our practice transactional rather than adaptive. If we are honest, these kinds of questioning interactions with learners tell us little to nothing about the conceptual understanding they are developing. They tell us nothing about how a learner has arrived at such a conclusion, what misconceptions they may have developed along the way or how their cognition is functioning in relation to such topics. Even worse, we may, through our ineffective questioning practice, fail to root out misconceptions and we may even further develop these.

— REFLECTIVE ACTIVITY —————————————————————

Let us take another example:

Teacher: Let's think about this question everyone. What is 10 x 8?

Learner: The answer is 80.

Teacher: How do you know that?

Learner: [Pausing] I added a zero on the end.

Based on this different interaction, what assessment information has been gained from this questioning exchange?

What would your own response be to the solution given by the learner of adding a zero?

How could we further improve this interaction to glean even more accurate and nuanced information?

TYPES OF QUESTIONING

To start developing an adaptive practice of questioning we must develop an overview of the different types of questions we may ask. A typology of questions can help us to not only develop our questioning, but also to plan for learning more carefully and respond to needs when they arise in a lesson. Some examples of the questions we might ask are included in Table 8.1. Whilst no question is necessarily better than any other, if we are to be responsive educators we need to understand the role of each type in learning. We also acknowledge that there are others who have developed further typologies of questions that you could explore (Worley, 2019). However, for the purpose of adapting learning, we have focused on a selection that can be practically and easily applied to a learning situation by a beginning or expert teacher. Not only this, but often we see questioning as a simple activity which is done during the lesson, with perhaps some slight planning beforehand. But the question remains: if we want to be an adaptive and responsive teacher, how can we ensure our practice of questioning is supporting this practice? Simply, we have to train ourselves to ask questions. We have to review and analyse our practice and make improvements.

Table 8.1   Question types and examples

Type of question	Example	Context
Enquiry	In what ways could we describe this character?	Questions that prompt enquiry and investigation into a topic as well as the gathering of information
Convergent (closed)	How many continents are there?	Questions which encourage single answers and typically have a restricted set of possible solutions

Type of question	Example	Context
Divergent (open)	How might we find out how …?	Questions which encourage open-ended thinking and exploration, and which generate a range of possible solutions
Conjecturing	Some say there are only five continents on Earth. What do you think?	Questioning where incorrect or incomplete information is offered for learners in a hypothetical or speculative manner
Recalcitrant	Why do you think that? Are you sure? How are you sure?	A line of questioning which, rather than offering a solution by the educator, encourages learners to generate their own answers through continuous requestioning
Cloze	The word 'frog' in this sentence is a _____?	Questions that ask learners to identify a missing aspect or part, and that draw attention to a certain learning point
Cognitive	What steps did you take to identify all of the adjectives in this paragraph? Could you use this method on this text also?	Questions that focus less on the knowledge or concept and more on the process of arriving at a conclusion. This could involve analysis, synthesis, evaluation, or application of knowledge to another context
Metacognitive	What steps did you take to arrive at that answer and how could you improve next time?	Questions that encourage learners to become aware of and analyse their thinking process, its strengths and weaknesses and how this can be improved
Socratic	Statement: climate change is a huge threat to humankind Question: what evidence supports this claim and are there any counter-arguments or alternative perspectives on this issue?	Questioning which considers a statement and encourages dialogue so that learners may come to the answer on their own

REFLECTIVE ACTIVITY

- Which of the question types in Table 8.1 do you think are most suited to an adaptive teaching classroom and which are least suited? Can you make a list in order of which might be most and least useful? What is the reason for this?

- Think of a lesson you will teach in the future. For each of the types of questions above, generate an exemplar question for the lesson you are going to teach. Use these questions in your lesson and then reflect on how successful they were in supporting learners to think deeply. Which questions were less successful in helping learners to do this?

RESPONSIVE QUESTIONING

As we have identified, too much of what we do in classrooms is focused on teaching and not on learning. When we shift our focus to learning, we can have a different viewpoint on this practice. Here we would like to explore what adaptive and responsive questioning might look like in the classroom. Firstly, we shall explore how teachers' questioning can become adaptive and responsive and, secondly, we shall explore student questioning and how we can support learners to use questioning for learning and not teaching.

TEACHER QUESTIONING

We believe teacher questioning should be a small part of the questioning taking place in the classroom. When it does happen, it should be adapted in four ways:

- *Person-focused*: questioning that is customised and responsive to an individual's background, experiences, or demonstrated knowledge. This ensures that the questioning is relevant and engaging for the person being questioned. As we discussed in Chapter 7 on Cognition and metacognition, we may also wish to adapt our questioning to the cognitive needs of the learners in our class. For example, we may have recently introduced a new topic to our learners and at this point they are starting to develop some understanding of new concepts. Therefore, it is important to adapt our questioning carefully to the general needs of the class. Asking very abstract questions which increase the cognitive load of our learners will likely be ineffective.

  Example: We may ask a different type of question based on our knowledge of our learners. We may alter the content of the question or the subject knowledge on which it is based. Equally, we may ask our learners to draw a comparison to their own personal lives and intellectual capital. In principle, our relationship with and knowledge of our students may dictate the questioning employed whilst maintaining high standards of each and every learner.

- *Learning-focused*: questioning which is less about solutions and more about the processes or procedures which have taken place to arrive at that solution. Remembering that sometimes we need to focus on the procedural aspects of learning rather the final result of such learning is important. This can be a big shift for our learners because if we have mainly focused on 'playing the game' of expecting answers, learners may be confused when we shift our focus away to *how* they reached such an answer.

  Example: We may ask our learners about the methodology, approach or process they have undertaken to produce a solution. Articulating how a learner has done something can provide a wealth of information and also show us the many different ways in which a learner may approach a method or process. It can also be an interesting exercise to collect all the different methods or procedures learners use to arrive at a solution.

- *Progression-focused*: questioning which focuses on pushing forward the understanding and learning of an individual. It focuses on growth and advancement of a concept or idea which has been built on another idea or concept. This type of questioning adapts over time and might also be considered as assessment for learning.

  Example: You may ask a learner a divergent question because you know they have some basic understanding of an idea. By asking them a divergent question, they can begin to think about this concept in different and varied ways. This will cause the learner to progress their thinking.

- *Feedback-focused*: adaptive questioning often involves providing feedback after each response. Positive reinforcement for correct solutions and constructive guidance for incorrect answers can enhance the learning or problem-solving process and involves a constructive dialogue, promoting a culture of continuous improvement.

  Example: Typically, future-orientated questions might be asked which focus on the steps that learners need to take to improve in the future. These could be performative (how they will achieve a better outcome), behavioural (how they might do something differently) or cognitive (how they might think differently).

STUDENT QUESTIONING

As we have argued, we believe there needs to be a shift in the quantity of questioning taking place in the classroom: fewer questions by teachers and more questions by learners. This will be of no surprise to early years practitioners, who actively encourage this kind of practice already. Young children have a plethora of questions to ask, often coined as the *why* phase in their development. But when do learners lose this love of questioning? Let's be clear, they do not lose it, they are educated out of it. Teachers ask questions and learners answer them. It is time we changed this. It has also become common practice in classrooms for learners to be encouraged to ask questions of themselves and other learners. Again, an experienced and confident teacher might see this as a perfect opportunity to engage learners. For a new teacher, this might be scary and unknown. It is difficult to control this kind of activity so many beginning teachers tend to avoid this strategy. Allowing learners to ask lots of questions shifts the power and autonomy of learning away from teachers and towards learners, but this allows the opportunity for different directions and tangents in the learning to take place. Below are two types of student questioning.

- *Self-questioning and metacognitive processes*: metacognitive practices help learners to question the processes involved in planning, monitoring and critiquing their other learning activities and actions. This is a huge topic and we have discussed many aspects of this in Chapter 7, focusing on metacognition and how this relates to a learner's cognitive processes.

Example: You may ask a learner to engage in a self-questioning process. This could be asking them to think about the efficacy of a particular method or procedure they have used to engage in a learning activity. Perhaps you ask them to reflect on planning a science experiment or how they produced a particular product in design and technology. By modelling this kind of self-questioning, learners will be become familiar with this as a natural process.

- *Questioning other students*: when a teacher asks questions, this can be effective but imagine a classroom full of learners asking each other questions! This would be a remarkable learning environment, one in which every member of the community asks questions. Of course, not only is this incredibly practical, we also know that when learners ask each other questions, this is much less high stakes and produces amazing results. In a classroom with one teacher, making every learner a teacher of another is a great way of producing a conjecturing atmosphere, reducing the pressure on teachers to be everywhere all the time. Putting learners in the driving seat of questioning their peers is incredibly effective and will hugely contribute to an atmosphere of questioning. Whilst this can be understood as peer assessment, in this context it is using peer questioning as a pedagogic strategy, one which increases learning and teaching.

Example: At the beginning of a lesson, you share what you wish the learners to focus on. Next you ask your learners to question one another on how they might go about doing this in the lesson. You give them a range of scaffolded question such as 'How will you approach this problem?', 'How are you going do this?' or 'How would you approach planning this investigation?' By doing this, as a pedagogic technique, we immediately place our learners in the place of teacher and encourage them to think about the process which they will use to engage in a learning experience.

ADAPTIVE RESPONDING

For effective adaptive learning and teaching to take place we need effective questioning as part of our adaptive learning and teaching toolkit. To do this we also need to stop playing the game of asking questions. If adaptive practice is also about learning rather than teaching, we need to ensure our learners are prepared to respond effectively and be responsive in these exchanges. It is a well-known fact that responding to questions is often a process where speed is of the essence. Cazden (2001) famously wrote that, on average, students are given a second or less to offer a solution to a question. Equally, they found that, counter-intuitively, more able students are often given more time to consider an answer whereas those who were deemed as less able were given less time! This shows there is something very wrong with the way in which our learners respond to our questioning. How do we change this? Simply, we need to teach our learners a new way of responding to questions.

To move learners away from the game of answering questions, we must give them a new way of speaking so they can adequately adapt and respond to our questions. We must teach them a new language which makes them also questioners. For many teachers this is a scary concept. You may be thinking, 'What if I do not know the answer to their question?' or perhaps 'I am going to look really stupid if I get this wrong in front of an entire class!' However, we have to remind ourselves that often the best learning takes place when wrong solutions are offered, or when there is not an immediate solution to a question. We have got to stop playing the game. Responding to such scenarios with statements like, 'I am not sure, but let's find a way to find out together ...' or even 'I think I am wrong here, what do you think?' can send a powerful message to our learners.

We need a strategy to enable to learners to respond as learners not as individuals playing a game. Here are some examples of responses that could be offered to learners in our class to enable them to actively engage in learning.

- *Conjecturing response*: conjecturing responses are ways for learners to test their ideas in relation to our teaching and learning.

  Examples: I am thinking this might be a solution. Am I going in the right direction?

  I think this method is wrong? Do you agree with me?

- *Clarifying response*

  Examples: Could you explain what you mean by that?

  I do not understand, can you change the way you are saying that?

  Can you show me a different way of trying to understand this?

- *Relationship response*

  Examples: How does this relate to what we were learning yesterday?

  Why is this important in this topic? I do not see how it connects.

- *Considering multiple perspectives*

  Examples: What might someone do differently when trying to solve this problem?

  Are there any other ways to approach this question? Can we make a list?

- *Prior knowledge response*

  Examples: How does this link to what we were learning in yesterday's lesson?

  How does this question connect to what you already know about the topic?

  Can you think of any similar problems or situations you've encountered before?

The examples above are just some of the ways in which we might encourage our learners to begin thinking about questioning. Again, if we think back to Chapter 4, Adaptable environments and experiences, we can regard ourselves as a teacher less as an expert who should know everything and more as an interventionist who is creating the right conditions for our learners. By encouraging this kind of practice, we are producing an environment that gives learners permission to question not only knowledge and ideas, but also us.

WRONG SOLUTIONS AND ADAPTIVE QUESTIONING

We wanted to finish this chapter by bringing your attention to the role questioning has in ensuring errors, misconceptions and bugs are identified, acknowledged and addressed in learning and teaching. It seems impossible to speak about questioning without discussing wrong solutions because it is one of the main tools we can use, both as a pedagogical and assessment strategy, to address misconceptions and errors.

As Jack has previously argued (Stothard, 2021), it is important, as learners and teachers, to clarify these terms. Words such as 'mistake', 'misconception' and 'error' have been readily discussed in a mathematics context but are less frequently used in other curriculum contexts. We must also remember that each of these words holds a different meaning which can powerfully affect learning and teaching in the classroom. It may be useful to remember a time when you were told you were wrong or that you made a mistake. Consider what effect this had on you as a learner or how you felt about learning itself. Too often, these words have negative connotations and can halt learning. Swann et al. (2012) helpfully argued that misconceptions are not 'wrong' but a natural stage in the development towards securing a concept. Therefore, moving away from the idea that making mistakes is a negative thing is complementary to the idea and concept of learning. Of course, we want all learners to develop a correct and secure understanding of concepts, but wanting to skip over the essential process of forming and rewriting over misconceptions is not only contrary to learning but impossible. Making 'mistakes' is not only seen as beneficial in learning but also as an essential aspect of the learning journey in all curriculum subjects.

However, learners do not always give wrong solutions due to misconceptions. We also have to factor in errors in the learning process. There is a subtle distinction here, but we can generally say that errors tend to revolve around procedural aspects of learning whilst misconceptions tend to focus on conceptual aspects of learning. Hansen (2020) has written extensively on this topic, specifically from the viewpoint of mathematics. Using her definition, we can think of errors as occurring for a variety of different reasons. Whilst these may relate to a misconception, they don't necessarily mean there is one. 'Errors' could hint at deeper issues in a learner's understanding of a subject area, but they may be nothing more than surface-level inconsistencies. Hansen has argued that errors in understanding can be as far-ranging as carelessness, a lack of concentration or a deeper conceptual issue.

CASE STUDY

Take the following example of Lena and David who are working on using capital letter in English:

Error: Lena is writing a report as part of an English topic she is working on. She is writing about her recent trip to a local zoo. She is working alongside other learners in this process and engages in dialogue and questioning with her peers. When it comes to her teacher to looking over her work, they notice that Lena has not used a capital letter for the name of the zoo. They question Lena about it and Lena immediately remembers that it is a name and needs a capital letter as it is a proper noun.

Misconception: In a similar case David is writing his own report about his visit to the zoo. In his report, the name of the zoo is sometimes capitalised but in other cases it is not. His teacher is concerned and asks him a question to find out about this error. David tells his teacher that the name of the zoo only needs a capital letter when it comes after a full stop. David knows the start of a new sentence needs a capital letter.

In the case study, we can see how questioning the learning identifies two different types of issue. In Lena's case, we can see this error was caused by carelessness because, when questioned by her teacher, she was immediately able to explain where she had gone wrong and made the correction. In David's case, it is clear he has a misconception around capital letters for proper nouns because, when questioned, he exposed his misconception around the use of capital letters. In summary, Lena had an error whilst David exposed a deeper misconception. However, in each case, the teacher was able to identify this due to their questioning. We must remember that when attempting to use questioning adaptively, learners may not present their misunderstandings so easily. It is possible that the conditions for certain misconceptions to become obvious are not always possible, which allows them to remain undetected for long periods of time. This can be very problematic for learning as students can go for many years without such misconceptions arising. In reality, wrong solutions tell us more about the understanding of our learners than correct ones do. On a procedural level, we begin to comprehend the processes and steps that our learners take in trying to reach a solution to a problem. Equally, wrong solutions give us valuable insights into the conceptual errors that our learners have developed.

USING QUESTIONING TO IDENTIFY ERRORS AND MISCONCEPTIONS

Here are some questioning strategies we can use to help identify errors and misconceptions in a learner's understanding:

- *Recalcitrant questioning*: whilst 'recalcitrant' can have negative connotations as a word, it can be extremely powerful as a type of questioning to address errors in understanding.

Here, by recalcitrant, we mean the type of questioning that continues to delve deeper and deeper into a learner's understanding, taking their responses and asking for further information, clarification or depth. Although this type of questioning can be challenging, it allows teachers and learners to see where there may be gaps or misconceptions in their thought processes and understanding. By continuously probing and testing a learner's responses it is possible to uncover deeper, underlying misconceptions or errors that it would not be possible to find out with only superficial questioning. By engaging in recalcitrant questioning, you are asking for greater clarification around an idea or concept and, as this develops, it is more likely that if a learner is holding a misconception, this will be manifested for you to identify. Over time, as you develop this type of questioning practice, learners will adapt to this acknowledging that, as a teacher, you will want more than a simple solution to a question you pose. It is also a powerful technique to teach your learners.

- *Reflective questioning*: throughout this book we have discussed autonomy and giving learners the power over their own learning. Asking learners questions which require them to reflect on the learning they are undertaking may be a powerful way of discovering errors and misconceptions. As we discussed in Chapter 7, Cognition and metacognition, when learners have experiences in which they moderate their own cognitive processes they are engaging in metacognitive activities. This can be crucial for uncovering misconceptions as it makes the learners discover this for themselves.

- *Peer questioning*: we know that when learners are questioned by each other, there is much less pressure for them to feel they must give a 'right' answer. As such, peer questioning is a powerful way to identify and address misconceptions in learning. When learners listen to one another and discuss what they are learning, they are able to access different perspectives. In this situation, it would be possible to scaffold the questioning, perhaps by giving them a copy of the questioning grid from earlier in the chapter. However, it is important that, as a teacher, you are tuned in to the conversations taking place in your classroom.

REFLECTIVE ACTIVITY

Plan to engage in this activity, which could be at the end of the day or perhaps in your registration time. Present the following terminology, as discussed above, to your class:

- error

- mistake

- misconception

- wrong.

Ask the learners in your class what they think the meanings of these words are. Perhaps, if appropriate, you could ask them what emotions or feelings these particular words bring up for them as individuals. As part of shifting your classroom culture away from mistakes and errors as negative to a place where they are valuable learning experiences, discuss how these are important aspects of learning. You could even use some of the examples given in this chapter to help.

FINAL THOUGHTS

As with each of the previous chapters, there is no end to our questioning practice, and we have argued that we must continuously train in developing our questioning if we want to be truly adaptive teachers. We have argued that the ubiquity of questioning in learning and teaching is both its strength and its greatest weakness. The saying 'the more you do something, the better you get' is challenged here as we know teachers often ask hundreds of questions daily but most of this practice is shallow and superficial. Equally, questioning is often unplanned and spontaneously takes place in lesson. As such, insufficient thought and planning goes into questioning practices, resulting in ineffective enquiring and the loss of many opportunities to deepen understanding. Moving away from playing 'the game' of asking and answering questions can be one of the most powerful ways of improving your pedagogical practice and learning culture.

Whilst we acknowledge there is no end to the types of questions that can be asked, we hope our typology of questions might be useful for developing your own bank of questions that you can actively use for planning your lessons and, more importantly, refer to in your lesson as you attempt to adapt your practice. Each type has its own strengths and limitations and should be used specifically for different types of situations. Over time, as you become more fluent and familiar with utilising effective and adaptive questioning, you will grow in confidence and notice yourself being more specific in the types of questions you ask. Finally, we have made a strong argument for the special role questioning has in identifying, acknowledging and addressing errors, misconceptions and bugs in the learning process. It will be important for you to think about the differences we have discussed in relation to mistakes, misconceptions and errors, acknowledging their impact on learning and teaching. The negative connotations often associated with these terms are important to acknowledge in an adaptive and inclusive classroom.

REFLECTIVE ACTIVITY

Lesson study is a Japanese instructional improvement strategy that can be a powerful tool to help teachers reflexively examine their own practice and enhance pedagogical practice (Godfrey et al., 2018). It focuses on teachers working collaboratively to plan, observe, analyse and refine lessons with the goal of improving teaching and student learning. Using the information in this chapter, plan a lesson in which the focus of your lesson will be questioning. Use the following steps:

(Continued)

(Continued)

1. *Collaborative planning*: plan your lesson thinking carefully about the types of questions you want to use and the learners in your class. You could plan a range of different questions, or perhaps focus in on a certain type of questing such as self-questioning on the part of your learners. Plan with a peer or colleague to help inform your decisions.

2. *Teach the lesson*: having planned your lesson, teach your lesson ensuring this is recorded or a colleague can observe you in a constructive yet critical way. If this is not possible, why not ask another adult in the classroom, such as a teacher assistant, to give you feedback. Make sure you and your critical friend pay close attention to students' reactions, engagement and understanding.

3. *Debriefing*: after the lesson, reflect on how effective the questioning was. Remember, the focus of this reflection should be how it helped you to adapt your practice to maximise learning in the classroom. You should discuss and reflect on what you and your critical friend observed.

4. *Refining*: having engaged in this process you are ready to plan for your next lesson. Work with colleagues or peers again to plan the next lesson, making refinements and adjustments to your questioning to further improve your adaptive practice and the quality of the learning in the classroom.

KEY TAKEAWAYS

- Do not play the game: as teachers we can get sucked into the practice of playing the game of asking questions and simply wanting a 'correct' answer. Whilst this may look good performatively, it is superficial and does not tell us a great deal about learning.

- Plan your questions like you plan every other aspect of your lesson, with precision. It may seem that leaving questions to chance in your lesson is an effective strategy, but it simply means that you will likely continue to ask the same types of questions as you always have. Spend quality time planning the types of questions you will ask as pedagogic and assessment tools.

- Let the learners take the lead on questioning. Remember, whilst it is important you utilise questions effectively, encouraging your learners to become budding questioners is crucial. A classroom filled with questioning learners is a classroom full of enquiry, conjecture and thinking.

- Teach learners how to be responsive to questions. We see so many classrooms filled with learners who simply guess what a teacher wants to hear and give that answer. Teach your learner to be responsive, asking you questions back for clarification and precision.

- Finally, and, in some ways, most importantly, teach learners that making a mistake is OK. We cannot overstate how important it is to create a culture in which learners feel it is OK to try out ideas with the possibility they can be mistaken. Teaching learners that they will likely develop misconceptions and make errors as they learn and that this is an important step towards precise concept acquisition is essential!

FURTHER READING AND RESOURCES

Hansen, A. (Ed.) (2020) *Children's Errors in Mathematics*. London: Learning Matters.

Mason, J. (2010) *Effective Questioning and Responding in the Mathematics Classroom*. Open University and University of Oxford. Available at: http://mcs.open.ac.uk/jhm3/Selected%20 Publications/Effective%20Questioning%20&%20Responding.pdf

Worley, P. (2019) *100 Ideas for Primary Teachers: Questioning*. London: Bloomsbury.

9

NON-CONCLUSION

This final chapter is called a *non-conclusion*. This is because we do not want you to view this as the end of your adaptive journey; rather, this is a starting point for you to gather the reflections that you have been prompted to consider throughout this book. It is now time for you to begin to move forward as a practitioner, taking elements of practice that you think could be adapted for your classroom and experimenting with different approaches.

Decide how you will begin; it could be that you choose a pedagogy from the flexible grouping chapter and embed one of the approaches into your planning sequence for an upcoming foundation subject topic, or you could choose to spend some time focusing on your questioning across the curriculum. Whatever you decide is right for you and your learners, be brave and have a go – adapt, tweak, restructure, reorganise – but set a pace that is achievable, realistic and, most importantly, prioritise being kind to yourself. It is important to remember that even one small change could make a significant difference.

The DfE's ECF (2019a) provides very key guidance for beginning teachers and their mentors to follow when discussing development against the key standards. With this in mind, we have taken each element of Professional Behaviours (Standard 8 – Fulfil wider professional responsibilities) and given consideration to how adaptive teaching can be interwoven into these areas successfully.

INVESTING IN YOURSELF AS A TEACHER

CCF 8: 'Effective professional development is likely to be sustained over time, involve expert support or coaching and opportunities for collaboration.'

In this book we have considered the various ways in which you can adapt your practice to become the best teacher you can be. However, we also recognise that it is important to spend time and effort investing in yourself as a teacher.

One aspect of this, and another reason why we have titled this chapter as the Non-conclusion, is that we want to foster a love of learning in ourselves. We want to develop a mindset of lifelong learning which is crucial to becoming an adaptive teacher. This can mean different things to different people. Embracing a mindset of lifelong learning also means you are open to change, which can often be a scary thing to face. Over time, there have been numerous changes and adaptations to the curriculum and how we go about teaching this and assessing it. As such, developing an open mind about these changes is crucial to becoming an adaptive teacher. We believe that empowering yourself with new knowledge and ideas is the best way to stay ahead of the curve in education. You can do this by actively engaging with research or simply reading something that interests you. Either way, it is about developing a curiosity about ideas that continue to be important in education.

CONTINUING PROFESSIONAL DEVELOPMENT

Continuing professional development (CPD) is an excellent way of continuing to update your skills. Whilst your university or school will undoubtedly have a range of CPD on offer for you, it is also about being curious and identifying where your own strengths and limitations lie and acting upon these. As we discuss below, reflecting on your own strengths and limitations can help you to become a better teacher for your learners. With education being a dynamic and changing field engaging fully with CPD can help you further develop your curriculum knowledge, pedagogical content knowledge and assessment practice. Equally, it can support you in developing your wider skills such as behaviour management and how to support the wider activities of your school.

Networking and collaborating outside your school can also be an excellent way of incorporating new and exciting ideas into your practice. There is a wealth of opportunities to explore, especially with the ever-expanding range of online materials available, many of them free to teachers. Why not see what free webinars and classes are available?

CURRICULUM AND SUBJECT KNOWLEDGE

Another crucial way we can invest in ourselves as teachers is by ensuring our curriculum and subject knowledge remains as secure as possible. By doing so, we can reduce our own unease and gain confidence that when teaching we have the expertise to be the best teacher we can. Teachers' Standard 3, 'Demonstrate good subject and curriculum knowledge' states that teachers should:

- *have a secure knowledge of the relevant subject(s) and curriculum areas, foster and maintain pupils' interest in the subject, and address misunderstandings*

- *demonstrate a critical understanding of developments in the subject and curriculum areas and promote the value of scholarship.*

Having a secure knowledge of the curriculum and the subject we teach will have many unintended consequences that will improve our adaptive practice. With expert curriculum and subject knowledge, we can be sure that our assessment of learners is consistent and realistic. We know what learners should know and how they will learn this, and we can design assessment opportunities much more easily. Moreover, our use of questioning will improve as we fine-tune our questioning and responses based on our knowledge of the curriculum.

MODELS OF REFLECTION AND REFLECTIVE PRACTICE

CCF 8: 'Reflective practice, supported by feedback from and observation of experienced colleagues, professional debate, and learning from educational research, is also likely to support improvement.'

One of the most challenging aspects of learning and teaching is the need to critically reflect on our own assumptions, thoughts and experiences. As a teacher, developing a range of techniques and practices to reflect on our experiences and those of our learners is crucial to becoming an adaptive teacher. Whilst there are many different models of reflection, two specific models are presented below which could be invaluable.

BROOKFIELD'S FOUR LENSES (2017)

In *Becoming a Critically Reflective Teacher*, Brookfield (2017) suggests that assumptions are a powerful way of shaping our thinking and behaviours. They originate from many sources – including our own personal experiences or those of trusted others. Thus, Brookfield states that critical reflection is 'the sustained and intentional process of identifying and checking the accuracy and validity of our ... assumptions' (p. 3). Whilst this model of reflection was designed to help educators think about the processes they undergo in their learning, it is applicable to any learner who is questioning their assumptions about a particular concept, topic, or experience. Thus, Brookfield's four lenses are as follows:

- *Students' eyes*: if we can see ourselves and the effects that our actions have on others, we can begin to question and clarify the assumptions we hold. We can, for example, question whether the meanings we assign to our actions are the same as those taken away by other individuals such as our learners. By collecting feedback from students, we can begin to interpret and understand further.

- *Colleagues' perceptions*: by engaging with colleagues in critical conversations and asking them to observe our behaviours and practices, we can access information that is normally hidden from us. Others can suggest alternative courses of action or ways of thinking about a situation. Thus, we can find new ways of developing and adapting our pedagogical and assessment practices.

- *Personal experience*: our personal experiences as teachers can unlock new ways of thinking. Take an experience as a learner in your classroom or your school and consider how you might use this to develop an understanding of what hinders or supports you as a learner. How could this experience be improved?

- *Theory and research*: finally, Brookfield suggests that academic literature can be a powerful way of illuminating and enacting critical reflection. Theoretical and research literature can shed new light on familiar scenarios and experiences. Theoretical models, such as the work of key theorists and thinkers, can offer an opportunity to explore and revaluate a common-sense practice or situation.

GIBBS' REFLECTIVE CYCLE (1988)

Critically reflecting on an experience can be difficult, especially in the busy life of a teacher. In the case of trying to become an adaptive teacher, there might have been a specific moment which made you decide to take the leap. This could have been as simple as a conversation or a life-changing event. Using Gibbs' (1988) reflective cycle, we can begin to critically evaluate experiences by engaging in six separate but linked phases. Gibbs pursued active experience in learning and argued that this should also be applied to reflection on experience. It allows for planning and future success as an educator. Gibbs (1988) proposes a reflective cycle comprising six stages which can structure a debriefing or critical reflection on an experience.

1. *Description*: What happened? Don't make judgements yet or try to draw conclusions; simply describe.

2. *Feelings*: What were your reactions and feelings? Again, don't move on to analysing these yet.

3. *Evaluation*: What was good or bad about the experience? Make value judgements.

4. *Analysis*: What sense can you make of the situation? Bring in ideas from outside the experience to help you. What was really going on? Were different people's experiences similar or different in important ways?

5a. *Conclusions*: (general) What can be concluded, in a general sense, from these experiences and the analyses you have undertaken?

5b. *Conclusions*: (specific) What can be concluded about your own specific, unique, personal situation or way of working?

6. *Personal action plans*: What are you going to do differently in this type of situation next time? What steps are you going to take on the basis of what you have learnt?

Gibbs' reflection cycle allows the exploration of various experiences more thoroughly and critically, both as a teacher and a learner.

CONTRIBUTING TO WIDER SCHOOL LIFE AS AN ADAPTIVE TEACHER

CCF 8: 'Teachers can make valuable contributions to the wider life of the school in a broad range of ways, including by supporting and developing effective professional relationships with colleagues.'

As a beginning teacher, it can be very easy to feel overwhelmed by the sheer complexity of the role. Imposter syndrome affects us all at some point, the feelings of 'how did I get here?' and 'should I even be here?' are something that I am sure you will experience at the start of your career. The key message here is that, as a practitioner who is at the start of their journey, you are best placed to be able to share new approaches with colleagues because you have most recently been trained. Your ITT/E programme will have supported you to consider the most recent research-informed practice; you will have investigated and read academic texts that outline suggestions for innovative and theoretically underpinned pedagogy; you will also have had the opportunity to work in a variety of school environments during your placements that will have enabled you to observe others in practice, no doubt 'magpie-ing' ideas and adapting them to suit your learners along the way. When working with colleagues, be open to being both supportive and supported. If you implement a new idea and you are happy with the outcome, share this with your colleagues, demonstrate how you implemented the approach and, importantly, demonstrate the impact that it has had in your classroom. Do not be afraid to share good practice; this is part of professionalism and you have a professional duty to contribute to the success of your school. Adaptive teaching is regarded by some schools as unclear and difficult to define; it is important to remember that policy shifts and those who trained years ago may not have taken the opportunity to really reflect upon alternatives to differentiation, for example. Often, beginning teachers focus too much on what a school can do for them, rather than what they can contribute to a school; we ask you to turn this around and make a difference.

WORKING WITH STAKEHOLDERS

CCF 8: 'Building effective relationships with parents, carers and families can improve pupils' motivation, behaviour and academic success.'

At the heart of this book, we have argued that the needs of each learner are the most important aspect of adaptive teaching. By extension, this approach will also recognise the importance of understanding the individual needs of each student's family and home situation. As teachers, we want our learners to grow and develop in a safe, happy and stimulating learning environment. By understanding this situation for each learner – not only in school, but also in their wider life – we can further understand and adapt our approach to learning and teaching, considering their nuanced experiences. We also want parents, carers and families to support us and feel supported as our learners develop through their educational journey. Through adapting our teaching, we can support the diverse needs of learners, which reinforces the relationship between school and the home. Therefore, adaptive teaching can help build strong relationships with parents, carers and families in the following ways.

HELPING US UNDERSTAND AND SHOW CULTURAL SENSITIVITY

When we recognise that learners can come from diverse socio-cultural backgrounds, we are better able to understand their learning needs. Therefore, adaptive learning and teaching should always be culturally sensitive. By acknowledging and respecting the cultural diversity within the student body and their families, teachers can foster stronger connections and develop connections between school and home. In turn, when learners recognise the strong bond between home and school, this can have a hugely positive impact on their own motivation and behaviour. A breakdown in communications and relationships between home and school often leads to poorer outcomes from learners, both personally and academically.

COMMUNICATING EFFECTIVELY WITH PARENTS, CARERS AND FAMILIES

Equally, we have a good understanding of adapting for individual learners; we will also have a good understanding of how we can adapt our communication, even with parents, carers and families. By becoming familiar with parents, carers and families we can ensure our communication is strong and effective. Many schools use a variety of methods and channels to ensure effective communication takes place so that strong and positive relationship can be fostered and developed. This also means that when challenging conversations need to take place, lines of communication are already open and functioning.

DEVELOPING SHARED GOALS AND TRUST

Because adaptive teaching focuses on aligning students' needs, adaptive teaching focuses on developing shared goals between school and parents, carers and families. When teachers and parents share commons goals and aspirations for their learners, it often leads to collaborative partnership which will have a positive outcome for students. For example, a common message from school and home can send a clear message to learners. Another unintended benefit of this process can be increasing levels of trust between schools, teachers, parents, carers and families. Open communication and a commitment to the wellbeing of learners develops relationships and trust. When parents, carers and families feel involved in the education of learners, it can have a positive effect.

WORKING WITH COLLEAGUES

Teaching assistants (TAs) can support pupils more effectively when they are prepared for lessons by teachers – and when TAs supplement, rather than replace support from teachers.

TAs are an invaluable and integral part of many settings; however, as explored in Chapter 6, Adaptive interventions, the deployment of support staff must be managed with care and consideration. As a teacher, it is your responsibility to ensure that all the learning and teaching that takes place in your classroom is of the highest quality and that the curriculum is accessible for all; it is not acceptable for the same learners to be segregated from whole-class learning daily.

As part of your professional commitment, it is essential that any members of staff who are supporting learners are adequately trained to deliver what is required and that effective dialogue is prioritised to ensure that formative assessment is shared effectively, next steps are identified and, ultimately, that children make progress. As a beginning teacher, it can be daunting managing staff who may have worked at a school for several years and are comfortable with the processes that may have been in place for some time. See any changes that you would like to implement as an opportunity and share it as such; demonstrate your acknowledgement of the wealth of experience and understanding that your colleague brings, and balance this with new ideas and approaches – develop a partnership, working together with the common aim of supporting all learners as effectively as possible. Introduce any changes to classroom practice with care, ensuring that everyone feels involved with the process and that you take the knowledge of others into consideration as this will show them that you value their input and expertise. The fear of the unknown is very real and can become a significant barrier to improvement and change. Your classroom is a micro-climate within the school, therefore be mindful of how your vision complements that of the wider environment and how other staff work together too.

SEEKING OUT EXPERT ADVICE

CCF 8: 'SENCOs, pastoral leaders, careers advisors and other specialist colleagues also have valuable expertise and can ensure that appropriate support is in place for pupils.'

As teachers, we can sometimes feel like we need to do everything ourselves. However, becoming an adaptive teacher means we should and must seek out guidance and support from our colleagues, especially those experts within our school community and further afield. Whether it is through working alongside or collaborating with experienced colleagues or attending conferences and training, we can gain valuable insights and knowledge from others. This is foundational for adaptive teaching because it ensures we have others to support us. Imagine you are faced with a new and challenging situation with regards to adapting your instruction. Seeking the advice of others is crucial because they may have faced such a situation themselves in the past and have good advice on how to move through it.

PLAN A CPD SESSION ON WHAT YOU HAVE LEARNT ABOUT ADAPTIVE TEACHING

CCF 8: 'Engaging in high-quality professional development can help teachers improve.'

The very fact that you have chosen to read this book demonstrates a commitment to finding out more about adaptive teaching; this will hopefully inspire you to try some of the suggested approaches shared in the toolkit. As a teacher, you will be offered formal professional development as part of your school training. This is usually informed by the action plan and areas for development will be identified by the school leadership team; it might also be that a subject leader delivers specific CPD to meet a wider school need.

Regardless of the intent, professional development is not only the responsibility of a setting, but also that of the individual teacher. As part of your ITT/E programme, you will have completed audits linked to your subject knowledge, for example; no doubt resources were signposted to support your confidence and knowledge in specific areas and you will have responded by spending time focusing on these areas. As a teacher, there are many demands on your time – the day-to-day running of a classroom is intense. However, we encourage you to remain research-informed and open to new ideas. When you have a problem to solve, use the skills developed over the course of your training to find a solution; keep updated with EEF blogs; and sign up to social media channels that specifically support aspects of learning and teaching with new ideas that are research-informed. Many charities and organisations offer support for professional development. If you have a particular interest in an aspect of the curriculum or a particular learning need, stay curious and explore how you can get support using a different approach; be open to new ideas and embrace the opportunity to refresh and revitalise your practice.

Ultimately, we hope that this toolkit will enable you to see yourself as an ambassador for adaptive teaching – you could lead some professional development linked to this approach. The tangram activity at the start of Chapter 3, Grouping, could be a great way to demonstrate the limitations of fixed grouping, for example. As we say to our beginning teachers before they embark on teaching practice: now go forth, and be the change!

SO, YOUR ADAPTIVE JOURNEY BEGINS ...

Imagine an adaptive classroom that is accessible and open to everyone. Think of this space as a community of learners in which everyone can learn, grow and achieve together.

Draw sketches of your ideas or make a list of what comes to mind when you think about an adaptive classroom environment.

Now look back at the sketches of your ideas or the list that you made of what came to mind when you thought about an adaptive classroom environment when you were first challenged to complete this task in the introductory chapter. Now that you have explored this book, how are you thinking differently about adaptive teaching?

REFERENCES

Alexander, R. (2020) *A Dialogic Teaching Companion*. London: Routledge.

Baines, E., Blatchford, P., Kutnick, P., Chowne, A., Ota, C. and Berdondini, L. (2008) *Promoting Effective Group Work in the Primary Classroom: A Handbook for Teachers and Practitioners*. Taylor & Francis: Abingdon

Bearne, E. and Reedy, D. (2018) *Teaching Primary English: Subject Knowledge and Classroom Practice*. New York: Routledge.

Blatchford, P. and Webster, R. (2018) Classroom contexts for learning at primary and secondary school: Class size, groupings, interactions, and special educational needs. *British Educational Research Journal*, 44, 681–703.

Boaler, J. (1997) When even winners are losers: Evaluating the experiences of 'top set' students'. *Journal of Curriculum Studies*, 29(2), 165–82.

Boaler, J., Wiliam, D. and Brown, M. (2000) Students' experiences of ability grouping: Disaffection, polarisation and the construction of failure. *British Educational Research Journal*, 26(5), 631–48.

Brookfield, S. (2017) *Becoming a Critically Reflective Teacher* (2nd ed.). San Fransisco: Jossey Boss.

Brown, A. and Campione, J. (1996) Psychological theory and the design of innovative learning environments: On procedures, principles, and systems. In L. Schauble and R. Glaser (Eds.), *Innovations in Learning: New Environments for Education*. Hillsdale: Lawrence Erlbaum Associates (pp. 289–325).

Brualdi, A.C. (1998) *Classroom Questions*. ERIC/AE Digest (ERIC Publications ERIC Digests in Full Text No. EDO-TM-98–02 RR93002002). Washington, DC: ERIC Clearinghouse on Assessment and Evaluation.

Bruner, J. (1964) The course of cognitive growth. *American Psychologist*, 19(1), 1–15. https://doi.org/10.1037/h0044160

Cazden, C.B. (2001) *Classroom Discourse: The Language of Teaching and Learning* (2nd ed.). Portsmouth: Heinemann.

Child, S. and Ellis, P. (2021) *The What, Why and How of Assessment: A Guide for Teachers and School Leaders*. Thousand Oaks: Corwin.

Coe, R. (2013) *Improving Education: A Triumph of Hope Over Experience*. Durham: Centre for Evaluation and Monitoring.

Department for Education (DfE) (2013a) *National Curriculum*. Available at: www.gov.uk/government/collections/national-curriculum

DfE (2013b) *National Curriculum in England: Primary Curriculum*. Available at: www.gov.uk/government/publications/national-curriculum-in-england-primary-curriculum

DfE (2015) *Special Educational Needs and Disability Code of Practice: 0 to 25 Years. Statutory Guidance for Organisations which Work with and Support Children and Young People who have Special Educational Needs or Disabilities*. Available at: SEND_Code_of_Practice_January_2015.pdf (publishing.service.gov.uk)

DfE (2019a) *Early Career Framework*. Available at: https://assets.publishing.service.gov.uk/media/60795936d3bf7f400b462d74/Early-Career_Framework_April_2021.pdf

DfE (2019b) *Initial Teacher Training (ITT): Core Content Framework*. Available at: https://assets.publishing.service.gov.uk/media/6061eb9cd3bf7f5cde260984/ITT_core_content_framework_.pdf

DfE (2021) *Teachers' Standards: Guidance for School Leaders, School Staff and Governing Bodies*. Available at: https://assets.publishing.service.gov.uk/media/61b73d6c8fa8f50384489c9a/Teachers__Standards_Dec_2021.pdf

DfE (2023a) *Special Educational Needs in England Statistics Report*. Available at: https://explore-education-statistics.service.gov.uk/find-statistics/special-educational-needs-in-england

DfE (2023b) *Suspensions and Permanent Exclusions in England: Autumn Term 2022/23*. Available at: https://explore-education-statistics.service.gov.uk/find-statistics/permanent-and-fixed-period-exclusions-in-england/2022-23-autumn-term

Department for Education and Skills (DfES) (2006) *Grouping Pupils for Success, Primary and Secondary National Strategies*. Crown Copyright. Available at: https://wsassets.s3.amazonaws.com/ws/nso/pdf/bbd59a99cf4ad4a66ac8a25069a72063.pdf

Deunk, M., Smale-Jacobse, A., de Boer, H., Doolaard, S. and Bosker, R. (2018) Effective differentiation practices: A systematic review and meta-analysis of studies on the cognitive effects of differentiation practices in primary education. *Education Research Review*, 24, 31–54.

Dyson, D., Dunne, M., Gallannaugh, F., Humphreys, S., Muijs, D. and Sebba, J. (2007) Effective Teaching and Learning for Pupils in Low Attaining Groups. Research report DCSF-RR011. London: DfCSF.

Education Endowment Foundation (EEF) (2018a) *Best Practice in Mixed Attainment Grouping*. Available at: https://educationendowmentfoundation.org.uk/projects-and-evaluation/projects/best-practice-in-mixed-attainment-grouping

EEF (2018b) *Education Endowment Foundation Teaching and Learning Toolkit*. Available at: https://educationendowmentfoundation.org.uk/evidence-summaries/teaching-learning-toolkit/

EEF (2021) *Making the Best Use of Teaching Assistants: Guidance Report*. Available at: https://educationendowmentfoundation.org.uk/education-evidence/guidance-reports/teaching-assistants

Equality Act (2010) Equality Act 2010 (legislation.gov.uk)

Flavell, J. (1979) Metacognition and cognitive monitoring: A new area of cognitive–developmental inquiry. *American Psychologist*, 34(10), 906–11.

Florian, L. and Black-Hawkins, K. (2011) Exploring inclusive pedagogy. *British Educational Research Journal*, 37(5), 813–28.

Garry, T. (2020) *Mastery in Primary Mathematics: A Guide for Teachers and Leaders*. London: Bloomsbury.

Gibbs, G. (1988) *Learning by Doing: A Guide to Teaching and Learning Methods*. Oxford: Oxford Brookes University.

Glazzard, J., Stokoe, J., Hughes, A., Netherwood, A. and Neve, L. (2010) *Teaching Primary Special Educational Needs*. London: Learning Matters.

Godfrey, D., Seleznyov, S., Anders, J., Wollaston, N. and Barrera-Pedemonte, F. (2018) A developmental evaluation approach to lesson study: Exploring the impact of lesson study in London schools. *Professional Development in Education*, 45(2), 325–40.

Hallam. S. and Ireson, J. (2006) Secondary school pupils' satisfaction with their ability grouping placements. *British Educational Research Journal*, 33(1), 27–45.

Hansen, A. (Ed.) (2020) *Children's Errors in Mathematics*. London: Learning Matters.

Hattie, J. (2012) *Visible Learning for Teachers: Maximizing Impact on Learning*. London: Routledge.

Hattie, J. and Larsen, S.N. (2020) *The Purposes of Education: A Conversation between John Hattie and Steen Nepper Larsen*. Abingdon: Routledge.

Hewitt, D. and Wright, B. (2019) *Engaging, Motivating and Empowering Learners in Schools*. London: Sage.

Luft, J. and Ingham, H. (1955). The Johari window, a graphic model of interpersonal awareness. Proceedings of the western training laboratory in group development. Los Angeles: University of California.

Mosey, C. and Stothard, J. (2022) Reimagining adaptive teaching: Creating a supportive environment for all learners. *IMPACT: Journal of the Chartered College of Teaching*, 15.

National Statistics (2023) *School Workforce in England, Reporting Year 2022*. Available at: https://explore-education-statistics.service.gov.uk/find-statistics/school-workforce-in-england

NRich (2019) *Creating a Low Threshold High Ceiling Classroom*. Available at: https://nrich.maths.org/7701

Ofsted (2019) *Education Inspection Framework: Overview of Research*. Available at: www.gov.uk/government/publications/education-inspection-framework-overview-of-research

Ofsted (2021) *Principles Behind Ofsted's Research Reviews and Subject Reports*. Available at: www.gov.uk/government/publications/principles-behind-ofsteds-research-reviews-and-subject-reports/principles-behind-ofsteds-research-reviews-and-subject-reports

Ofsted (2023a) *Education Inspection Framework*. Available at: www.gov.uk/government/publications/education-inspection-framework

Ofsted (2023b) *School Inspection Handbook*. Available at: www.gov.uk/government/publications/school-inspection-handbook-eif/school-inspection-handbook-for-september-2023

Palaiologou, I. (2019) *Child Observation: A Guide for Students of Early Childhood*. London: Learning Matters.

Papert, S. (1980) *Mindstorms: Children, Computers and Powerful Ideas*. New York: Basic Books.

Roberts, J. (2016) The more capable peer: Approaches to collaborative learning in a mixed ability classroom. *Changing English*, 23(1), 42–51.

Shepherd, A. (2018) *The Boy Who Grew Dragons*. London: Piccadilly Press.

Shulman, L. (1986) Those who understand: Knowledge growth in teaching. *Journal of Education*, 193(3), 1–11.

Smit, J., van Eerde, H. and Bakker, A. (2013) A conceptualisation of whole-class scaffolding. *British Educational Journal*, 39(5).

Stothard, J. (2021) Identifying hidden misconceptions in mathematics. *Mathematics Teaching*, 37–9. Available at: https://atm.org.uk/Mathematics-Teaching-Journal-Archive/177010

Swann, M., Peacock, A., Hart, S. and Drummond, M. (2012) *Creating Learning Without Limits*. Maidenhead: Open University Press.

Tarrant, P. and Holt, D. (2016) *Metacognition in the Primary Classroom: A Practical Guide to Helping Children Understand How They Learn Best*. London: Routledge.

Taylor, B., Francis, B., Archer, L., Hodgen, J., Pepper, D., Tereshchenko, A. and Travers, M. (2016) Factors deterring schools from mixed attainment teaching practice. *Pedagogy, Culture and Society*, 25(3), 327–45.

Tomlinson, C.A. (2001) *How to Differentiate Instruction in Mixed-ability Classrooms*. Alexandria, VA: ASCD.

Tomlinson, C.A. (2014) *The Differentiated Classroom: Responding to the Needs of All Learners*. Alexandria, VA: ASCD.

Training and Development Agency (TDA) (2008) Special Educational Needs and/or Disabilities: A Training Resource for Initial Teacher Providers: Primary Undergraduate Courses. Available at: https://webarchive.nationalarchives.gov.uk/ukgwa/20101007140523/http://sen.ttrb.ac.uk//viewarticle2.aspx?contentId=15002

Van de Pol, J. Volman, M. and Beishuizen, J. (2010) Scaffolding in teacher–student interaction: A decade of research. *Education Psychology Review*, 22(3), 271–96.

Vygotsky, L.S. (1978) *Mind in Society: The Development of Higher Psychological Processes*. Cambridge, MA: Harvard University Press.

Warnock, H.M. [Warnock Report] (1978) *Special Educational Needs: Report of the Committee of Enquiry into the Education of Handicapped Children and Young People*. London: HMSO.

Wass, R. and Golding, C. (2014) Sharpening a tool for teaching: The zone of proximal development. *Teaching in Higher Education*, 19(6), 671–68.

Wood, D., Bruner, J. and Ross, G. (1976) The role of tutoring in problem solving. *Journal of Child Psychology and Child Psychiatry*, 17, 89–100.

Worley, P. (2019) *100 Ideas for Primary Teachers: Questioning*. London: Bloomsbury.

Wray, D. and Lewis, M. (1997) Teaching factual writing: purpose and structure. *Australian Journal of Language and Literacy*, 20(2).

INDEX

www.ingramcontent.com/pod-product-compliance
Lightning Source LLC
Jackson TN
JSHW062325310126
97517JS00011B/113